Bernard J. McQuaid

Christian Free Schools

Bernard J. McQuaid
Christian Free Schools
ISBN/EAN: 9783744725392
Printed in Europe, USA, Canada, Australia, Japan
Cover: Foto ©ninafisch / pixelio.de

More available books at **www.hansebooks.com**

CHRISTIAN
FREE SCHOOLS:

OR,

THE RIGHT OF PARENTS TO PROVIDE RELIGIOUS EDUCATION FOR THEIR CHILDREN, WITHOUT LET OR HINDRANCE.

THE SUBJECT DISCUSSED

BY

B. J. McQUAID,

BISHOP OF ROCHESTER

FREQUENT requests for copies of the following lectures which could not be furnished because not in print, have suggested the advisability of publishing in book form the two lectures given in Rochester and the one in Boston, together with articles which appeared in the NORTH AMERICAN REVIEW and the FORUM.

The aim of the author has been to address an audience of his fellow American citizens, as an American speaking to Americans, on a subject of importance to all classes in the community, and that concerns even the future welfare of the Republic. It has not been his purpose to assail State Schools, or Schools without religious instruction and enforcements, for those who prefer such schools, much as he may lament the absence of the religious element; nor has he sought to limit or impede the spread of education among the people. His purpose has been to uphold the rights of parents who seek for religious instruction, training and enforcements in the schools to whos care they entrust the education of their children.

It is quite possible to arrange a system of State Schools, and another of parental Schools, which will secure to each all just demands, without the sacrifice of inalienable rights. As a help to a proper understanding of the question these pages are presented to the consideration of their readers.

The authorities quoted in these papers are for the most part American and non-Catholic. These, more than the ablest Catholic theologians and writers, are likely to enlist attention.

Political parties are responsible for much of the misconception existing in the American mind with regard to the attitude of Catholics toward State Schools. The lessons of the last Wisconsin election, and the statistics of schools, public and private, as found in the census of 1890, are grave studies for politicians and others.

Religious bigots who assert that our liberties and government are in danger from Christian Free Schools and the Catholic religion, are not deserving of notice.

In the hope that the facts and arguments here presented may help remove unnecessary fears and apprehensions, and demonstrate to our American fellow-citizens that the ambition of Catholics is to further the cause of the people's education, without doing wrong to any class in the community, a respectful hearing is asked.

FIRST LECTURE.

(As reported for the Union and Advertiser, December 9th, 1871.)

In Corinthian Hall last evening, in response to the invitation of a large number of our citizens, Bishop M'Quaid discussed the question of Popular Education from a Catholic standpoint. About half-past six o'clock the people began to assemble, and before half-past seven, the hour announced for the commencement of the discourse, the Hall was literally jammed and the doors had to be closed, leaving a large crowd outside unable to gain admission. Such was the pressure that the drop curtain had to be raised and the theatrical stage in the rear of the lecturer's desk given up to those who could find sitting or standing room upon it. No admission by the doors was possible after half-past seven, and many hundreds who came to hear had to go away without hearing. The disappointed, however, will find their satisfaction in reading at their leisure the full report of the UNION given below.

At the appointed time Bishop M'Quaid made his appearance upon the rostrum accompanied by a large representation of our American, German and Irish Catholic fellow-citizens, including some dozen or more of the clergy of those nationalities. There were also upon the stage as listeners several Protestant clergymen, one at least of whom took occasion at the close to declare his hearty concurrence in the demand for Christian free schools. Owing to the crowd and the efforts to pack the vast audience into the best shape possible, it was long before sufficient order could be obtained to enable the Bishop to proceed. And not till he had spoken some time did perfect quiet prevail. The time occupied in delivery was two hours; and during the delivery repeated rounds of applause attested the fact that the assemblage was decidedly in accord with the Bishop's views.

Bishop M'Quaid spoke as follows:

My best thanks are due to the gentlemen whose invitation has given me this opportunity of addressing my fellow-citizens on the all important subject " Christian Free Schools."

Some estimate may be formed of the importance of the subject from the fact that there are in the State of New York one million five hundred thousand children of school age; as also from the vast pecuniary interests at stake, as the State alone in its Public and Normal Schools, Academies, and for educational purposes, expends more than ten millions of dollars annually; whilst the Universities, Colleges, Christian Free Schools and private schools of every description disburse a sum of money running into millions.

Pecuniary considerations, however, dwindle into insignificance when comparison is made with those higher interests that concern the future welfare, prosperity and permanence of our Republican institutions. A people who are to govern themselves need virtue and morality much more than intellectual knowledge to appreciate and preserve the form of self-government. Hence it is so truly said that a Republic needs moral and virtuous citizens.

Influenced by motives of political self-preservation the various States of the Union have sought from time to time to devise and establish systems of common schools for all their children. With the consent of a majority of the people, common schools for secular education, as it is called, have been organized in all the States.

New York State has as general, broad and liberal system of Public Schools as any other in the Union. Whilst the system of schools now existing has many opponents, some of whom deny the right of the State to educate children any more than to feed and clothe them, the vast majority concede the right to the State to impart an intellectual education to all who choose to avail themselves of the boon.

There are two points almost universally accepted. The first is the primary and natural right of parents to procure for their children the best education they can, (and no education is worth having that leaves out religious culture,) and their duty to guard and protect the minds and hearts of their offspring, in their years of tender and confiding trustfulness from every danger to morals, virtue and good principles.

The second conceded point is the want of right in the State to interfere in the religious teaching of parents or children, confining itself strictly and solely to secular knowledge, and excluding absolutely all religious instruction.

We shall see before the close of this address that when the State professes to impart an education purely secular and free from all religious teaching she lays claim to do an impossible thing; that if she could give such an education it would be a great misfortune to the children, to the family and to the State; that the attempt to do it is doing great harm, and inflicts great injustice upon those parents who are hindered by the interference of the State from providing for their children the description of religious training which best enables them to satisfy the dictates of conscience.

The present system of Public Schools in this State professes to exclude all religious exercises. We are often told that this is the American system, and that it is very impertinent for foreigners to wish to bring religion into schools against the American idea. So far as any system of public schools can be said to have an American idea, the idea will be found to be " Education based on religious instruction."

The first schools established in New York City and in many places of the State were religious denominational schools. These schools were supported by the churches with which they were connected and by their patrons. Religious exercises formed a part of the daily duties of the class room. The early founders of this Republic were not able to understand how they could bring up their children in the knowledge, love and service of God by banishing the Bible, prayer and religious exercises of every kind from the school. Hence religion was reverenced and its duties attended to in all institutions of learning in the country. The American system of education in its incipiency, and for a long while, was one founded on Bible teaching and religious exercises. The present system is un-American, anti-American.

In the year 1805 some benevolent gentlemen of New York City seeing that many children did not attend any of the Parochial schools, came together to establish a "Free school for the education of such poor children as do not belong to or are not provided for by any religious society." The first schools of this new organization were put in operation by the generous contributions of benevolent individuals, but their benevolence soon took the form of taxation and from helping in the cause of education they soon absorbed, through State support and generous taxes, all schools of their standard, effectually crushing and driving out of existence the Parochial schools which they had been formed to assist. As in the earlier days, a great deal of religious teaching was given in the schools of the Public School Society, the various denominations of the city did not object strenuously to this gradual absorption of Parochial schools into the monopoly of the Public School system. Indeed the first free schools provided for the religious instruction of the children through the instrumentality of the different sectarian denominations of the city.

Prayer, Bible reading and the singing of religious hymns formed part of the exercises of the public schools of New York until 1840, at which time began the famous discussion "on the rights of Catholics in relation to the public schools." Besides, in those days, the attacks upon Catholics by the teachers and pupils were frequent and annoying; the reading books contained much that was offensive to Catholics, who, few in number and poor in this world's goods, were looked upon almost with contempt and were barely tolerated. They had only a small number of schools of their own, and perhaps not over five thousand children in Catholic schools in the entire State. I may here remark that the German emigration had scarcely begun at that date.

Before the controversy had got fairly under way, and before the violent and fanatic bigotry of the masses had been excited, Gov. Seward in his annual message to the Legislature, in 1840, inserted these remarkable words:

"The children of foreigners, found in great numbers in our populous cities and towns, and in the vicinity of our public works, are too often deprived of the advantages of our system of public education, in consequence of prejudices arising from difference of language or religion. It ought never to be forgotten that the public welfare is as deeply concerned in their education as in that of our own children. I do not hesitate, therefore, to recommend the establishment of schools in which they may be instructed by teachers speaking the same language with themselves and professing the same faith."

Gov. Seward speedily gave way before the clamor and misrepresentations that assailed him. His motives were kind and just; his views were correct; but he was in advance of the people.

John C. Spencer, Secretary of State, described by S. S. Randall, in his history of the "Common School System," as a remarkable man, " possessed of transcendent intellectual endowments and unimpeachable moral worth, * * * possessed of a mind gigantic in its comprehension and microscopic in its accuracy," made a report to the Legislature of 1841, in which, whilst stating clearly and boldly the difficulties of a general system of education in a community divided up into many religious denominations, gave the only solution that is possible:

" On this principle of what may be termed *absolute non-intervention* may we rely to remove all the apparent difficulties which surround the subject under consideration. In the theory of the Common School law which governs the whole State except the city of New York, it is fully and entirely maintained; and in the administration of that law it is sacredly observed. No officer among the thousands having charge of our Common Schools thinks of opposing by any authoritative direction respecting the nature or extent of moral or religious instruction to be given in our schools. Its whole control is left to the free and unrestricted action of the people themselves in their several districts. The practical consequence is that each district suits itself, by having such religious instructions in its school as is congenial to the opinions of its inhabitants.   *   *   *   If there is not entire fallacy in all these views—if the experience of twenty-five years derived from the school districts of the interior is not wholly worthless—then the remedy is plain, practical and simple. *It is by adopting the principle of the organization that prevails in the other parts of the State*, which shall leave such parents as desire to exercise any control over the *amount* and *description* of religious instruction which shall be given to their children, the opportunity of doing so. This can be effected by depriving the present system in New York of its character of universality and exclusiveness, and by opening it to *the action of smaller masses*, whose interests and opinions may be consulted in their schools, so that every *denomination* may freely enjoy its '*religious profession*' in the education of its youth."

These wise, statesmanlike and truly American views of John C. Spencer had to give way before the ignorance and religious bigotry then dominant in the State. Whenever a time comes for the settlement of the school question upon an equitable basis we shall have to go back to something like what John C. Spencer proposed in 1841. Instead of leaving the control of schools to parents, the State has stepped in as absolute master, monopolized education by levying ten millions of dollars to be used in its own way, in its own schools, driven away almost all competition and trampled down unfeelingly the humble endeavors of poor parents, who, in this land of freedom and equal rights, presume to educate their loved ones with that "*amount and description of religious instruction*" which conscience tells them is good, expedient, necessary.

And now that the common school system has triumphed over every competitor and ten millions of dollars are annually expended for educational purposes, what is the education which the State offers its children?

I shall ask two State Superintendents of Public Instruction to answer that question. Their authority will not be disputed.

Henry S. Randall, in his report to the Legislature in 1854, wrote:

" In view of the above facts, the position was early, distinctly and almost universally taken by our Statesmen, Legislators and prominent friends of education—men of the warmest religious zeal, and belonging to every sect—that religious education must be banished from the common schools, and consigned to the family and the church. If felt that this was an evil, it was felt that it was the least one of which the circumstances admitted. Accordingly, the instruction in our schools has been limited to that ordinarily included under the head of intellectual culture, and to the propagation of those principles of morality in which all sects, and good men belonging to no sect, can equally agree. The tender consciences of all have been respected. We have seen that even prayer—that morning and evening duty which man owes to his Creator—which even the pagan and savage do not withhold from the gods of their blinded devotion—which, conducted in any proper spirit, is no more sectarian than that homage which constantly goes up from all nature * * *
has been decided by two of our most eminent superintendents as inadmissible as a school exercise within school hours, and that no pupil's *conscience* or *inclination* shall be violated by being compelled to listen to it. * * * I believe that the holy scriptures, and especially the portion of them known as the New Testament, are proper to be read in school by pupils who have attained sufficient literary and mental culture to understand their import. I believe they may, as a matter of right, be read as a

class-book by those whose parents desire it. But I am clearly of the opinion that the reading of no version of them can be forced on those whose conscience or religion objects to such version."

This very year a gentleman residing in one of the neighboring villages of this county, whose child had been made to stand outside the school room, during the reading of the Bible, because it objected to that reading, appealed for justice to Mr. Weaver, the present Superintendent of Public Instruction, and received the following answer:

"ALBANY, February 11, 1871.

SIR:—The laws of this State do not require pupils in the Common Schools to participate in religious exercises of any kind, and neither teacher nor trustee has power to compel any pupil to unite in such exercises. According to the construction of the law established by the Department many years ago. the teachers may engage in such exercises before or after school hours, with such pupils as choose to attend. See Code of Instruction, 349, 354. Your obedient servant,

ABRAM B. WEAVER,
Superintendent."

The New York *Tribune* of November 25, 1869, in replying to an attack of the *Episcopalian*, would give up the Bible in New York city, where the law seems to permit its reading, as the only means of defending the Common School system against the assaults of Catholics.

As I prefer to let others speak, it will be pleasant to hear what a secular newspaper has to say of a system of education that dispenses with prayer. the reading of the Bible except as a class book for its *literary* merits, and religious exercises of any kind.

The New York World, September, 1871. commenting on a remarkable address of Gov. Brown, of Missouri, says:

" The truth is that the mistake of means in our system of education arises from a perversion of ends. On account of the recency of its establishment our school system answers much more nearly than those of older countries to what are considered by the majority of modern men the chief end of man in our time. That end is to get on in life; to make money, and to gain what money brings. To that purpose the present system is entirely adequate. * * * Human happiness is no longer defined in the words of the Catechism, 'to glorify God and to enjoy him forever,' nor even 'to live through the whole range of faculties,' but to get a fortune. * * * And our present system of education is thoroughly fit to attain it. To turn the hearts of the whole community from its present courses Mr. Brown and his co-workers will find to be a long job; but until it is done a right system of education cannot be established."

There is a picture of the education furnished by the State of New York to its children. It is calculated to show them how to get and spend money; and its highest morality is some worldly wisdom culled from old Pagan authors, or a literary class-book called the Bible.

Down to these depths of religious degradation have the Christian people of the State fallen. We Catholics believe that they forsook their earlier system of education to keep us from its advantages and to hurt our church. They have hurt themselves as Christians and honest men; they have emasculated education of all that gives it vitalizing power; they have helped to place the canker-worm of infidelity in the body politic, through the children; we have suffered in a pecuniary way, and because, like good citizens, we suffer when the country suffers.

Let us now examine the subject under another aspect. The present system of Godless education has been fastened on the State by the religious people of different denominations. Surely we shall find the principle of "education without religious instruction" a cardinal one in all the Protestant churches.

Alas! theory and practice are not always in accord. I shall, therefore, be obliged to exhibit to you the sad spectacle of preaching going one way, and practice suiting itself to circumstances.

The preaching of the leading men in the churches of the country is excellent, and its application to the higher classes is the same; they preach differently to the poor. Here are my authorities:

Thirty presidents of American colleges assembled at Oberlin, Ohio, to attend the second annual meeting of the Central College Association, an organization designed to promote collegiate and higher education, and destined to operate in the Western States, and I think down as far as Tennessee. Ex-President Finney—to Americans this gentleman is well known—addressed the meeting and laid down the principle that "religion must be taught. The highest judicial authority had decided the Christian religion to be the religion of the land." At the close of the session they passed three resolutions, two of which I will give you:

"Resolved, That we note with pleasure the evidences of increasing interest in the literary, scientific, and especially the religious education of the youth of our land; believing, as we do, that education not based upon Christian truth is of questionable value.

"Resolved, That we commend these interests to the sympathies, prayers and liberality of Christian people and congregations, that our schools may be increasingly useful as fountains not only of sound instruction but also of earnest, elevated piety."

I wish you to notice that the testimonies I am bringing forward are principally from men high in their churches, in charge of colleges and busy in educating the children of the wealthy. But, if the children of the wealthy, whose parents have education, have time, have means at home to attend to their religious instruction, need all the religious training that is here spoken of by these gentlemen and by others, how much more do the children of the poor, the children of the masses, the children of the American people, need it? They who are gathered into our colleges and universities, are but a handful compared with the millions covering the land that are to be found in our schools and places of elementary learning.

Dr. Anderson, President of the Rochester University, a gentleman whose life has been devoted to the training of young men, who stands high in his profession in this city in which he lives, and whose reputation as an educator is known I might say all over the country—a man who has a wonderful gift, as I understaud, of influencing the minds of others; who can draw young men to him, who can fashion and direct their ways of thought, who can mould and form their characters, Dr. Anderson, one of the first men in the Baptist Church in these United States, addressing the Baptist Educational Convention in the city of New York, says:

"Happily, I need not say much upon the subject of moral and religious education in colleges. By far the larger part of our colleges have been founded by religious men, and by prayer and faith consecrated to Christ. * * * I would only call attention to that kind of moral and religious influence which may be called spontaneous or incidental."

He speaks now of colleges and universities. Ten times more do we need such teaching in our schools—down where the people are, than in our colleges where the select few of the rich are to be found. Again he says:

"With the element of Christian faith in head and heart, *it is impossible for an earnest teacher to avoid giving out constantly religious and moral impulses and thought. He must of necessity set forth his notions about God, the soul, conscience, sin, the future life and Divine Revelation.*"

I endorse most heartily these correctly expressed views and sentiments of Dr. Anderson. They show how profound, how deep is his knowledge of the boy heart, and how well he understands the influence that must of necessity go out from the mind and the heart of every earnest teacher to work upon the plastic and susceptible hearts and minds of his young pupils, fashioning and forming them for their future welfare in the world. The Doctor goes on:

"If he promises not to do so he will fail to keep his word" —these are true words—or his teachings in science or literature, or history will be miserably shallow and inadequate. Our notion of God and the moral order form, in spite of ourselves, the base line which affects all our movements and constructions of science, literature and history. Inductions in physics, classifications in natural history, necessitate a living law, eternal in the thought of God. * * * All instruction unfolding the laws of science, literature and history should be permeated with the warmth, and light and glory of the Incarnate Redeemer."

"Incidental Instruction!" Here is the power of the teacher. The fact is, if you take a number of boys to instruct them, and dose them too largely with set forms of religion, you will do them harm. But if you go to work in Dr. Anderson's way—by incidental instruction—you may be sectarian, but you will make your scholars religious and just what you please:

"Incidental instruction in morality and religion, then," says the Dr., "ought to be the main reliance of the Christian Teacher. *The ends of a Christian school while working by its own laws and limitations, ought not to be essentially different from a Christian church.*"

Note well these words of the Doctor which I repeat:

"The ends of a Christian school ought not to be essentially different from a Christian church."

I would like to ask here what we shall call those schools that are not Christian? Can a school be called Christian in which all religious exercises are forbidden? The Doctor continues.

"The principles we have thus indicated are universal in their application. If the Christian teacher must make the elements of his religious faith color all his teaching, the same must be true of the unchristian teacher. * * * There is no good thinking that is not honest thinking. There is no good literature or art which is not the spontaneous outflow of the deepest elements of the moral and intellectual life. *If parents wish their children* educated in Christian principles, they must seek out honest, Christian men to be their Teachers."

I thank God that put it in the mind of Dr. Anderson to give such clear testimony in favor of sound Catholic views with regard to the education of the young.

There is nothing like variety.

You have heard the testimony of the thirty presidents and then that of Dr. Anderson, and now we shall give ear to B. Gratz Brown, Governor of the State of Missouri, a great politician and statesman. You will notice that these gentlemen are speaking on occasions when loose talking will not answer. Dr. Anderson addressed the Baptist Educational Convention; the thirty presidents of colleges were united at a Teachers' Convention. They are men advanced in years, of serious thought, speaking on serious questions, and their words are not to be taken lightly, like those of the writer in a newspaper who has to throw off his column per day.

Gov. Brown addressing the seventh National Teachers' Convention in St. Louis in August last, said:

"It is a very customary declaration to pronounce that education is the great safeguard of republics against the decay of virtue and the reign of immorality. Yet the facts can scarcely bear out the proposition. The highest civilizations, both ancient and modern, have sometimes been the most flagitious. Now-a-days, certainly, your prime rascals have been educated rascals."

I know you would be angry if I said this, but I am merely quoting from this gentleman, and if you go to Auburn, Sing Sing and other prisons, and examine some of the criminals confined there, you will find that there is truth in the Governor's words. Again:

"And it is at least doubtful whether education in itself, as now engineered, and confined merely to the acquisition of knowledge, has any tendency to mitigate the vicious elements of human nature, further than to change the direction and type of crime."

That is, without this education the crime might be of a low, mean and sensual order, but the educated criminal has attained a higher grade of crime. And again:

"This is not alleged, be it understood, of moral culture or religious instruction, but simply of the education of the intellect as it really obtains. * * * I say therefore, frankly, that whilst an earnest advocate of education, believing that knowledge is power, confessing that true advancement can only repose upon education, yet it is only a self delusion to mis-state the question and blind our eyes to what it does effect, by claiming for it what it does not by any necessity accomplish."

This speaks for itself and I need add nothing I strayed off from my regular authorities this time in quoting Governor Brown; now we will return home and call before us the Rev. Dr. Peck, President of the Board of Trustees of the Syracuse University, just at your door, and a gentleman well-known all through this part of the country, Addressing the East Genesee Conference at the city of Elmira, August, 1870, he says:

"The hope of our country is the Christian religion, the putting of it where it is not, and the allowing no man to take it away from where it is."

Very plain Anglo Saxon that:

"I charge not upon the Cornell University that it is infidel; but I state the fact. It has chosen its own ground. It is *negative* in religion."

And because it is negative it is therefore infidel, according to Dr. Peck. Evidently they are not teaching Dr. Peck's form of Christianity at Cornell University.

"Our institution is for positive Christianity, such as comes from the Holy Bible, such as Methodists will approve; that which will influence your children to come to Christ."

I like that plain Anglo Saxon style.

"If you want anything else don't put me on the Board of Trustees, nor ask me to give anything. These are your principles. God forbid that you should change them or seek to adjust them to the liberal religion of the day."

And this is the ground upon which the Syracuse University has been established — " opposition to the liberal religion of the day." Yet we American, Irish and German Catholics must send our children to schools negative and infidel in their teaching, or pay double taxes. Oh, no! Dr. Peck, of the Methodist Episcopal Church, has given us the right views, and we hold to them.

But he is not alone in his position.

The Rev. Dr. Steele, Vice-President of the Syracuse University, in his inaugural address in Syracuse August 31st, 1871, declaring to Syracuse and the country the intent and purposes of that University, and the mode of instruction to be followed there, spoke as follows:

"A far more important and much discussed question is the relation of University culture to religion."

And we poor people who belong to the crowd are told that we must lay aside religion, which must not enter into our education. Yet young men who have left their mothers' apron-strings, and are able to do for themselves, need the restraining influences of religion, need direct Christian teaching in order to make them good men; but the poor —let them go to their schools and be infidels if they have a mind to:

"We are not disposed to evade a question so vital, nor do we wish to assume any equivocal attitude before the public on this subject. Here we do not wish to innovate upon the general usage of American colleges which has prevailed with scarcely an exception from the day that Harvard opened its doors to the sons of the Pilgrims, 235 years ago,"

Rev. Dr. Steele here tells us that the prevailing usage of American colleges for the last 235 years—and very few of us wish to go back any further than that—has been to join secular education and religious culture :

"This mother of our colleges, by the appointment of a chaplain and by his required attendance upon daily prayers and public worship twice upon the Sabbath, reflects the almost uniform practice of the Universities and Colleges of our country. * * * It has been found that those who have been trained under the influence of mere mundane motives by the exclusive development of the earthward side of their nature to the neglect of the spiritual part, and by the use of ideas devoid of the high spiritual qualities which religion affords, have been destitute of that strength, symmetry, beauty and usefulness which made the lives of those who have thrown open the skylight of the soul, the spiritual nature to the transfiguring power of religious truth and spiritual influences, and who have been moulded by a culture vitalized and guided by the spirit of God.

"In the second place it is requisite to true culture by the aid which it affords to the moral of the student. There are systems of religion in which morals are divorced from religion. Such is not christianity. * * * So long as the Bible is the acknowledged foundation of our civilization, our civil and criminal codes of law, and so long as its spirit and teachings are requisite to the existence of self-government and of free institutions, it should have a place in the common school, the high school, the seminary, the university, as an influence necessary to conserve good order and pure morals.

* * * * *

"In the third, religion is necessary to culture by the aid which it affords."

Now, you will notice that this school question has great difficulties in it, and what is wanted is that we come together, discuss them, and if possible, find a solution of them. I desire with all my heart the substantial welfare of the people, and the permanence of this form of government. We cannot have any other form of government—no other would do in this land of ours, and my whole soul is in its success and stability, and I feel anxious and uneasy when I see principles laid down and systems taking deep root among us that are derogatory to a republican form of government, and are likely in future to do harm.

I may fatigue you with long readings from others, but I desire this evening to bring out the sentiments of very estimable gentlemen—ministers, college presidents and editors—on the necessity of religious education in schools and colleges.

The Journal of Commerce, of New York, thirty years ago, was the strongest and most violent opponent of Catholics in asking for their rights in this matter of school education. The Journal of Commerce of 1870 is quite another paper, although as staunchly Protestant as ever. In an article bearing date May 11, 1870, after saying that Catholics would not be satisfied with the exclusion of the Bible from the common schools, it asks:

"Would it satisfy Protestants? For ourselves we frankly answer no! Our first and chiefest objection sprang of the growing inattention to the religious culture of the young in their daily lesson in the class."

Yet we hear it said continually that children go into the class room merely to learn reading, arithmetic, geography, &c., and here we have the sentiments of the Journal of Commerce, a most able and influential paper, the writers of which are men of thought and education, who carefully weigh what they say—showing that religion must go into the daily recitations of the class. The article continues:

"Where the common school system won its chiefest laurels, and achieved its highest success, all scholastic learning was based upon the fundamental truths of religion, and the Gospel teachings were the only sanctions of faith and practice. The dissenters were so few in numbers that their rights were never respected, and the great majority being substantially of one faith consented to this sectarian intolerance. The system was wrong, because if the support came from the State bound to universal toleration, it ought not to force any religious system upon the child of a single objector; but the method was right, because without the sanction of religion there can be no proper training of the young in any branch of instruction; and the school where this is excluded is a heathen nursery. It is all in vain to say that geography, arithmetic, grammar, history, botany, &c., may be taught as sciences without any necessary connection with religion true or false ; and that the baptism of faith can be given to all these acquirements by exercises in the family and at the church, having no mutual relations with the school room."

All these gentlemen—Dr. Anderson, Dr. Peck, Dr. Steele, and the thirty presidents—tell us the same story with regard to the rich; and if the rich with all their advantages of books, many intellectual and moral associations, pleasant friends and instructive conversation, the family's minister visiting their homes, listening to eloquent discourses in the church, &c., if, with all these advantages the children of the rich, even in the study of botany and the sciences, need religious culture, need the "incidental instruction," spoken of by Dr. Anderson, how much more is it needed by the laborer's child, whose mother rises early in the morning and toils for her family while others are still in their beds, who, when the school hour comes, hurries off her child with scarcely time to say "God bless you ; " who, all day long labors on, busy in many ways to keep things together and eke out a bare subsistence ; whose father, in summer's heat and winter's cold, the year in and the year out, for some paltry pittance of a few shillings, in health or failing strength, like a machine that must stop only when it is worn out, works from morning until night, and has, perhaps, neither time, nor strength, nor patience to sit down with his children to supply the deficiencies and short-comings of the school and church?

It is the children of these poor people, who will make or mar the future of this mighty Republic. They constitute the numbers, they bring vigor and brightness of intellect, as well as strength and endurance of body to make powerful and energetic, if not virtuous and God fearing citizens. How, I ask, can these children find in the dingy apartment called their home, from such toil-worn and harassed parents, that amount of religious culture and instruction, which the State says shall not be given in the school, and which these gentlemen, speaking candidly for the members of their own churches, say, is essential for the education of the young? The article continues:

"The mind is not governed by laws which allow for such separations and distinctions."

"Good men will come to acknowledge this in time and will see that instead of excluding the Bible from the school, the great need of the race is in its systematic daily study in the formation of mind and character. * * * As Protestant from the most earnest convictions, we believe that nothing has contributed so much to the extension of the Roman Catholic organization and influence in this country, as the partial persecutions it has received from those conscientiously opposed to it.

"Give Catholics their full rights; ask nothing of them you would not willingly concede if you were in their place."

Just what we are standing before the whole world to-day asking for.

"Extend to them even a liberal courtesy, as believing that if they hold to some errors, they are not heathen or infidel."

We are Christians, we believe in Christ, we believe in the Bible as a divinely inspired Revelation, we believe in One God and Three Divine Persons, we believe in the Incarnate Redeemer; that Christ our Lord gave His blood to save us; we believe in heaven and hell, and a world to come; we believe in sin—and now pray tell us what else the Protestant believes?

In my anxiety to show that Catholics are not alone in regarding as defective and faulty the education given in the Common Schools, because separated from religion, I must beg your patient attention to another distinguished authority. This time it is no other than Dr. Coxe, Bishop of the Protestant Episcopal Church in Western New York. In a book called "Moral Reforms," page 135, he lays down the following positions as the proper ones to be taken by the members of his denomination. With the assistance of Dr. Coxe, and the entire Episcopal Church following the lead of their Bishop in favor of Christian schools, our holy cause must necessarily make great headway.

These are the positions to be held by churchmen, according to Dr. Coxe:

"I. Secure to every human being the best education you can provide for him."

Let the very beggar in the streets of your city have the best education you can provide for him, but because he is poor do not tell him to be content with stones when he asks for bread. Let our country be able to say to the world that it is a land in which no one, rich or poor, is left without the very best education that can be provided for him:

"II. Where you can do no better utilize the common schools, and supplement them by additional means of doing good.

"III. But where you can do better, let us do our full duty to our own children, and to all children, by gathering them into schools and colleges thoroughly Christian."

Many of the Presbyterians agree with Dr. Coxe on this question of Christian schools. In 1850 Rev. Mr. Young, pastor of the Presbyterian congregation in Warsaw, N. Y., wrote to Mr. Morgan, superintendent of common schools:

"The Presbyterian congregation, in this town, regarding the State plan of common school education as incompetent to secure that moral training of their children which is indispensable to a proper direction and use of the intellectual faculties—established, some eighteen months since, within the bounds of School District No. 10, a parochial school, to be instructed by such teachers only as profess religion. * * * In the progress of our school we find that evangelical religious truth sanctifies education as well as all other things with which it is connected; and that our children have made more rapid and effective progress in intellectual attainments than formerly but the 'Free School Law' passed by our last legislature has invaded our sanctuary, and we fear is about to thwart our purposes.

"We might have supposed that these principles of toleration which secure to the religious denominations respectively the privilege of worshiping God according to their respective views, and which excuse them from supporting those of a contrary belief, —that these principles would at least allow them the same toleration in the education of our children. But such toleration is now by legislative enactment denied us; while we are subjected to such onerous taxes for the support of common schools as are equivalent to an actual prohibition from carrying out our views, conscientiously entertained."

To quiet Rev. Mr. Young and the Presbyterian congregation of Warsaw, the superintendent of schools judged it expedient in reply to say:

"Shall the great body of Roman Catholics in the State be exempted from *their* share of the general tax for the support of Public Free Schools, aud the money raised upon the residue of the taxable property of the State be paid over to teachers employed by *their* respective churches, whose duty it shall be to 'incorporate into their system of daily instruction' the peculiar tenets of *their* religious faith."

We have listened to the utterances of distinguished men in the leading Protestant denominations, and if we take up the statistics of educational establishments in the country, we shall find that all the denominations of Christians are putting forth great exertions to found and endow Universities, Colleges, Seminaries and Academies—institutions for the higher studies of the wealthier classes. Catholics also found and establish Colleges and Academies for the rich members of their church, but their principles are as good and applicable for the poor as for the rich. Here is where we find the difference between them and the various Protestant denominations.

Whilst the latter have written wisely, learnedly and beautifully on the absolute necessity of religious instruction in schools and colleges where the young are to be educated, they make the application of their principle only in behalf of their rich communicants. Catholics, on the contrary, have put forth their strength in behalf of their poor children. These need religion and all its helps in the church, and at the fire-side, but still more in the school which is the *child's church.*

There are at the present time not far from one hundred thousand Catholic children in the Christian Free Schools of the State of New York, and there are over four thousand children in the Catholic schools of Rochester. These children are the children of the people; among them are children whose fathers' bones lie bleaching on the battle fields of the late war. Among them are many whose mothers' little earnings can ill be spared from the family's support.

If to-day we have one hundred thousand children in our schools, ten years hence that number in all probability will be doubled. For the past thirty years, since the first serious discussion of the right of religion to be in the schools, when we had very few Catholic schools in the State, we have been too busy providing church accommodation for our ever-increasing members to give that earnest attention to our schools which they merit.

In the years to come we shall be more occupied with school building and with the education of our children than the erecting of churches, although this work will not be permitted to stand still.

A plan or system of schools which excludes one hundred thousand children of the very classes in whose behalf Free Schools are supposed to be maintained, cannot be said to be a success. Schools that are carried on upon a basis so thoroughly defective as these in this city of Rochester, which are able to gather within their walls no more than 5,500 children in daily average attendance, whilst a portion of its citizens, who are unwilling to separate religion from education, can show an average daily attendance of 4,000 in special schools of their own, can scarcely be called Common Schools for all.

It is, we know well, the system which the majority of our fellow-citizens have adopted, but we have yet to learn that majorities, even if all-powerful, are infallible, or that minorities have no rights, or that a system that falls back in its ultimate defense when logic, sound sense and fair play have stormed all its positions, on the mere power of numbers, is a system that deserves to be permanent.

Much is said about *sectarianism, sectarian schools and sectarian institutions.* Indeed, you have only to mention the name to disturb the equanimity of many of our worthy fellow-citizens. It is singular how little attention they have given the subject, and how completely, blinded by the prejudices and feelings of their early education, they lose sight of reason, sound logic and fair play.

Two authorities will suffice to show what is truly meant by sectarian.

My first authority is John C. Spencer, Secretary of State and Superintendent of Schools, who in his report to the Legislature of New York in 1840 said :

" To this plan objections have been made that it would enable different religious denominations to establish schools of a *sectarian* character, and that thereby religious dissensions would be aggravated, if not generated. It is believed to have been shown that there must be some degree of religious instruction, and that there can be none without partaking more or less of a *sectarian* character ; and that even the Public School System has not been able, and cannot expect to be able, to avoid the imputation. *The objection itself proceeds on a sectarian principle,* and assumes the power to control that which is neither right nor practicable to subject to any domination. *Religious doctrines of vital interest will be inculcated,* not as *theological exercises, but incidentally, in the course of literary and scientific instructions;* and who will undertake to prohibit such instruction."

" It is believed to be an error to suppose that the absence of all religious instruction, if it were practicable, is a mode of avoiding sectarianism. *On the contrary, it would be in itself sectarian; because it would be consonant to the views of a particular class, and opposed to the opinions of other classes.* Those who reject creeds and resist all efforts to infuse them into the minds of the young before they have arrived at a maturity of judgment which may enable them to form their own opinions, would be gratified by a system which so fully accomplishes their purposes. But there are those who hold contrary opinions; and who insist on guarding the young against the influence of their own passions and the contagion of vice, by implanting in their minds and hearts those elements of faith which are held by this class to be the indispensable foundations of moral principles. This description of persons regard neutrality and indifference as the most insidious forms of hostility. It is not the business of the undersigned to express any opinion on the merits of those views. His only purpose is to show the *mistake of those who suppose they may avoid sectarianism by avoiding all religious instruction.*"

Another who has discussed this question of sectarianism with force and great plainness of speech, is the Rev. Dr. Spear of Brooklyn, in the columns of the Independent, thus:

" It is quite true that the Bible, as the foundation of religious belief, is not sectarian as between those who adopt it; but it is true that King James' version of the Holy Scriptures is sectarian as to the Catholic, as the Douay is to the Protestant, or as the Baptist version would be to all Protestants, but Baptists. It is equally true that the New Testament is sectarian as to the Jew, and the whole Bible is equally so as to those who reject its authority in any version. * * * There is no sense or candor in a mere play on words here. It is not decent in a Protestant ecclesiastic, who has no more rights than the humblest Jew, virtually to say to the latter: 'You are nothing but a good-for-nothing Jew; you Jews have no claim to be regarded as a religious sect, or included in the law of State impartiality as between sects which Protestants monopolize for their special benefit. Away with your Jewish consciences. You pay your tax-bills and send your children to the Public Schools and we will attend to their *Christian* education.' It is not decent to say this to any class of citizens who dissent from what is known as Protestant Christianity. It is simply a supercilious pomposity of which Protestants ought to be ashamed. It may please the bigotry it expresses, but a sensible man must either pity or despise it. In the name of justice we protest against this summary mode of disposing of the school question in respect to any class of American citizens. It is simply an insult."

We are frequently told by our non-Catholic friends that really we have no just cause of complaint; that if the State takes our taxes, it gives us in exchange schools for our children to which we can send them, if we please, that if we do not choose to patronize these Public Free Schools, we have no one to blame but ourselves.

This argument is readily accepted by those whom it suits. It does not answer us. In the first place, if we are not to go back to the days of pagan Sparta and resign all control of our children to the State, it will not be denied that parents have the natural right and duty to provide for their children the best education they can. Not many will question this right and duty; it is generally acted on by all parents who have the means to pay taxes and at the same time provide education, other than State education, for their children in seminaries, colleges and private establishments, in harmony with the religious views and wishes of their patrons; it is acted on by others, not so able to bear double taxation, but who are willing to make great sacrifices to fulfil a conscientious duty. There are others who are not able to provide for their children the kind of education which they would wish to give their offspring, because the State intervenes, and by taking a portion of their small resources, and by establishing with a lavish expenditure of the public funds, rival and competing schools, has rendered well nigh impossible the fulfilment of a bounden parental duty, and to this extent, is guilty of a gross wrong to many of its citizens.

There are citizens then who complain with truth and reason on their side that the legislation of the State operates unfairly and wrongfully, depriving them of equal rights. They might provide for their children the kind of education they deem suitable, and they, and not the State, are the judges of what that education ought to be, if the State did not tax them for the education of other people's children, or, if the State did not put religion under a ban and interdict, and make laws discriminating in favor of education without religious instruction, and against the efforts of its poorer citizens who prefer education with all the helps, influence and sacred spirit which religion alone can give.

The men who are advocating the establishment of Colleges and Universities for the training of Baptists, Episcopalians, Presbyterians and Methodists, surely will not discountenance the humbler efforts of their poor fellow citizens who seek for their children in the simple week-day school, that religious knowledge joined to secular learning, which alone gives hope of forming the character to morality and virtue.

What is good and useful in the College, is good and useful in the School; what is right for the rich is right for the poor. No rich man loves his child with more fondness, nor seeks its future advantage for this world and the next with more sincerity than does the plain mechanic, or humble laborer in his simple cottage.

The fallacy of unsound argument is in time detected by the people, and the play upon words, under cover of which many are deceived, ceases to avail.

Hence, whilst for a long time, *sectarianism* meant only Catholicism, and could be used as a battle cry to rally the unthinking or malicious bigotry of the crowd, now that it is coming to mean any aspect of religious teaching, or the plain reading of the Bible, without note or comment, sensible men will begin to ask, "Where is this going to end?"

I have never yet heard an honest argument to disprove or invalidate the views of John C. Spencer or Rev. Dr. Spear on this question of sectarianism. And I have no hesitation in asserting that the sectarianism prevailing in the public schools of this State is as objectionable to a large class of citizens as any other form of sectarianism that could be introduced.

It is the sectarianism of no religion, of infidelity; it is the sectarianism of those who have no form of religious belief, or are indifferent to all forms; it is a sectarianism that being in a majority plays the tyrant with fearful injustice. Listen to its cry which it passes for an argument: "If we give these religious people what they want, if we help sectarian schools, in their sense of sectarianism, what is to become of us?"

It was the sectarianism of no-religion which broke down the religious denominational schools in New York city, and all over the State in the first years of this century. And it is the religious people of the different Protestant denominations who with one breath blow hot and cold knowing that education without religious instruction is harmful, and yet trembling lest such a true doctrine might help the Catholics.

Here are two resolutions passed by a Convention of Methodist ministers held at Syracuse, this very week:

" Resolved, That we, as a convention, insist upon the *moral element* in the instruction afforded in our common school system, and especially the teaching of the moral system of Bible Christianity, which is the foundation of our civil law.

" Resolved, That the time has come when the constitution of the State of New York should be so amended as to prohibit peremptorily the appropriation by State or municipal authority of public funds for the support of sectarian schools, and we hereby solemnly and urgently petition the next Legislature to inaugurate the action by which this amendment may be secured."

To understand what these gentlemen of the Methodist Church mean by the *moral element*, and the *teaching* of the *moral system* of *Bible Christianity*, we must listen to the explanations given by these same reverend gentlemen. Rev. Mr. Jones, of Ilion, said: "Our right to sustain and control them [the public schools] was found in their Christian origin. He argued that moral culture must come from drill, and this must be given in childhood and in school. After a passing denunciation of political corruption, he said the teacher would not have to deal with the intellect alone. The state, in assuming to act *in loco parentis*, could not refuse to take care of the spiritual education of the children. Teachers must not be allowed to substitute the demoralizing doubtings of irreverent speculation for the grand saving truths of divine inspiration, whose essentials long ago became, and by the blessing of God shall continue to be the unwritten creed of this great American people."

Dr. Peck is already on record. He wants none of your milk-and-water Christianity—your liberal religion that means nothing; he wants the religion that will bring men to Christ—the religion that will suit the Methodists.

At this same Convention in Syracuse, Rev. Mr. Taylor ventured to say that Methodists did not wish to teach religion in the common schools, but, upon being taken to task for the utterance of such a heresy, and it was called a heresy by two of his brother ministers, he quickly explained and joined hands with Rev. Mr. Flack, who said that if the terrible heresy presented by Mr. Taylor should prevail, he would not hold his place a day as principal of a place of learning.

There is great confusion of ideas in these resolutions and speeches of the Methodist ministers. They call for a constitutional amendment to prohibit the giving of money to sectarian schools, and at the same time, and in the same breath, insist that the public schools shall teach religion, Bible Christianity, etc. To clear up the difficulty, to get at what is in their minds, substitute *Catholic* for *sectarian* and you will let in a ray of light, if not of honest-mindedness.

And so, in this whole controversy, from its origin to this day, whenever you hear a religionist of any kind speaking of sectarianism, when you reach what is in his mind, you discover that it is the spectre of Catholicism that frightens him.

After what you have heard from me this evening, many may be anxious to know what do these Catholics really mean, and what is it they want—what are their views upon this great subject of education. In the first place, we are in favor of education for the people. We are in favor of the most general system of education that can be devised. We favor a system that will bring in all the children of the State. But we do not favor a system that gives them a defective, injurious, poisonous education. Hence, since under the present system formed by the State we cannot take our stand upon the platform with our fellow citizens, we retire to one of our own. We build school houses and establish schools. I think that here, in this city of Rochester, we need not fear comparison with the public school houses of the city. Here are the two school houses of St. Joseph's, the largest school houses in the city; the school house at the Cathedral on Frank street; the very large and beautiful school house of St. Peter's congregation; and the not so large but more beautiful school house of the Immaculate Conception. We build school houses, large, spacious, roomy, well ventilated, well provided with all the appliances for imparting instruction. We supply teachers and books. And I would not fear, although in these schools religion holds the first place, like a beautiful goddess presiding over all—I would not fear to bring out the children of all these schools and place them side by side with the children of any other schools in the city for examination in those secular branches which we are told are so valuable. We know their value. And while these branches are studied in our schools, we wish to bring in the beautiful handmaid of religion to help the child and improve its mind, to mould its young heart, and to draw the mind and heart to God. Our schools furnish the children all the other schools do, and, furnishing this education, doing the very thing for which the State collects taxes and supports schools, we ask, and rightly and justly we ask, why it is that the money must all go in one direction and none of it come where so many of the children are to be found receiving the education the State means they shall have, and receiving at the same time that interdicted thing called religion? But whilst we claim these rights for ourselves we are equally strong in our convictions that the same rights belong to others. That whilst we bring religion into our schools and mean always to have religion there, we say to our non-Catholic fellow-citizens, bring into your schools whatever of religion you have—bring in prayer and religious singing and Bible reading. These means of good you hold as sacred and precious; we would much prefer good Protestants of any kind to infidels and deniers of all revelation; we thank God for any and all truth, wherever we find it. If but the beginning of truth to-day, we pray God that this small beginning of truth may grow into the fullness of all truth.

I do not propose to tell my fellow-citizens of this State this evening how they are to meet this subject. Little by little, next year, ten years hence if you please, the question will be settled upon a fair and just basis, without any more of those disastrous compromises which in the past have made the subject so difficult. Among those who have their children in our schools are foreigners from all the countries of Europe—Germans, and Swiss, and French, and Irish. These people come here to a land of liberty, and we tell them what a glorious country it is; and we can never exaggerate in praising the beauty, glory and advantages of this noble country. We tell them of all its many blessings ready for every poor down-trodden European who comes to our shores. But when these foreigners come they bring with them their consciences - they bring with them the religion in which they were born and educated, and that religion they prize more than the advantages the country offers, that religion they prize beyond all earthly gain. Shall we tell them that when they come to this country they may look after their own religion as they please in their own churches, but their children the State will take care of, and the State will see that no religious instruction is given them? Some of them come from Prussia, where the State most cautiously guards the religious interests of all. There are schools for Catholics and in those schools religion is attended to with the greatest care under the supervision of the parish priest. There are Protestant schools and the children are carefully instructed and trained in their religious duties by the ministers of parishes to which they belong. There the Jews have equal advantages. In republican Switzerland we have the same wise, just and equitable arrangment. In great Britain these schools for all kinds are favored and encouraged by the government. In Ireland, it happened that years ago, in those earlier days when the poor people were trying to emerge from a slavery of hundreds of years, they gladly accepted any boon of education the government gave them, and the government gave them one very much like the one we have in this country, secular education without religion—religion before and after school hours, but no God in the school. And this very year, almost this very month, although all through the land there were none but Catholics, the teachers and children Catholics, because God had been told to stand at the door of the school house, the Bishops of Ireland have passed condemnation upon these schools, and they insist that the schools shall be schools in which shall be found the cross upon which their Saviour died—schools in which the exercises may be opened in the name of the Father, the Son, and the Holy Ghost, in which the children may go upon their knees and adore the great and good God that made them.

I am not here this evening to find special fault with the common schools on any other score than the single one of banishing religion from them. If I were to do so I might take up the statement of Prof. Agassiz. Not many papers care to publish it. It is too terrible a thing to state.

But people say, "If you Catholics have schools, and our taxes go there, we shall be supporting Popery." I would like to know who pay the taxes. I always thought when the tax gatherer came around, he did not stop long to examine whether the dollars were Catholic or Protestant. That objection, I think, amounts to but very little. If the taxes do help us in our

Catholic schools, perhaps it will be the Catholic money that comes there.

Now what is the meaning of my speaking here this evening? I came here as an American citizen, speaking to American people. I have no other country. I come before the American people loving the country as dearly as any one else can. No one ever traveled through Europe who held his head higher and with more pride, or who more frequently spoke out in praise of this country than I did when there a year ago. After my God and my religion, my country is the dearest object of my life. I feel to-night in my heart the blot and disgrace that is upon the country by the wrong and unjust system of public schools that is now upheld in the land simply and solely by the power of the majority. I do not wish to say a single unkind, hard or threatening word. I come this evening to ask a fair discussion—to ask my fellow citizens to look at this great question without prejudice, without bigotry, having dispelled those unfortunate clouds that have been in their minds for so many years past. If no discussion can be permitted—if from first to last we can hear but the words, "we will it, we have made the law and the law shall stand, and the might of the majority shall prevail in spite of justice and of truth," then I would say that ten or twenty years hence the issue will not be with the gentlemen from Ireland and Germany, although their right to stand here is as good as the right of any man in the country—the issue will be with the children of these men from European countries. They are the children we are educating in our schools--into whose minds and hearts there will be planted deeply the true American feeling and principle that whilst they ought always to be good and law-abiding citizens they ought also to cherish with all the power of their souls the thought and the feeling that they should not submit to injustice or wrong one day longer than is absolutely necessary. It will be an unfortunate condition of things if this great and vital question of the education of the people finds no solution through reason, common justice and fair play, but must abide as it is until the majority is found on the side of justice and right. And whenever that majority—when the youth of to-day, come to be the men of ten years hence, you will find that American and Irish and German Catholics, on this question, will stand as one man in defence of their rights, in claiming them, in asking for them, and by those means which the constitution and the laws of the State place in their hands, in obtaining them. But how much better for us all to come together, brothers as we are, in this mighty and glorious country which the good Lord has given us, and discuss these matters—talk them over, without permitting prejudice and bigotry to stand in our way; for if they do stand in the way, they will stand in the way of the glory and stability of this country whose future God only knows. It is the duty of all citizens to labor with a good heart, a clear mind, an earnest soul, to do all they can in buildiug up and strengthening, and making still more glorious, this great American people.

SECOND LECTURE.

[*As reported for the Union and Advertiser, March 16, 1872.*]

A PLAN OUTLINED FOR STATE CONTROL AND SUPERVISION OF COMMON SCHOOLS IN HARMONY WITH PARENTAL PREROGATIVE.

Bishop McQuaid delivered last night in Corinthian Hall a second lecture on the question of Popular Education, a full report of which is presented below. This lecture is supplemental to the former one, and outlines a plan which would restore State education to the original limits of the Common School, and, while ensuring State control and supervision, would be in harmony with parental prerogative. This plan is understood to be acceptable to the large body of citizens and tax payers who protest against and will not use, even though compelled to pay for, the present system, and it is deserving of respectful and serious consideration. The two lectures, it was announced, will immediately be published together in pamphlet form.

Bishop McQuaid spoke as follows:

Whilst seated in this Hall a year ago, listening to the silvery tones of Wendell Phillips declaiming upon the power of the pulpit, the press and the rostrum, my mind was struck by the picture which he drew of the capabilities of the latter to educate the people.

There are questions which touch conscience most deeply and belong of right to the pulpit, but which under certain aspects may be more fitly discussed in the Hall than in the Church. Of this nature is the subject now under consideration.

As an American citizen I again stand before my fellow citizens to examine, discuss and agitate a subject which concerns the State in its corporate organization as well as each individual member thereof. The discussion and agitation demand calmness, plain talk and fair play. When the agitation ends in a settlement, that settlement will be based on truth, equal rights and common justice. If in the intervening years between the present moment and that time of settlement, be they few or many, some disputants should forget their own dignity, or the respect due to others, every outburst of temper, misrepresentation, or dealing in abusive and vulgar language will recoil upon the offender. Thank God it is characteristic of the American people to treat with disfavor the unfair and ill-tempered controversialist who misrepresents or distorts the facts and arguments of his opponents.

So far as the comments of the press elicited by the lecture on "Christian Free Schools" have come under my notice, there is no reason for complaint on personal grounds, however much the writers may have failed to argue against the positions taken in the lecture, contenting themselves with reiterating the determination of the American people to maintain the school system just as it is in spite of all that can be said against it. The newspapers have at least a vague perception that Catholics are citizens, and that in time their rights as such may come to be recognized, and when recognized may be found to be equal to those of other classes of citizens.

Some of the ministers of churches in this city in total forgetfulness of Christian Truth and Charity, have labored to show forth how bitter and spiteful are sectarian hate and jealousy. My work is not with such men, and dismissing them and their whole budget and bundle of futile topics and questions as in no way appertaining to the subject now before us, it is sufficient to say that their arguments and statements will be in order whenever the right of Catholics to live in these United States comes up for serious discussion.

In pleasing contrast with such ebullitions of uncharitableness are the fair, calm and sensible utterances of other ministers in this city and elsewhere. They do not agree with us on all points, but they give expression to their dissent in the language of gentlemen; they give the non-religionist the hope that all Christian pulpits are not given over to gall and bitterness and all manner of unkindness.

Thanking editors and ministers for every fair statement and every honorable attack made on the positions taken in the lecture on "Christian Free Schools," I proceed to explain my views more fully, and mark out more accurately and strengthen the positions already taken.

Fault has been found with the lecture because it did not lay down a plan of Common Schools to be established in place of the existing system against which such weighty objections are brought. The object of that lecture was to show serious and radical defects in the present system. Just now it is more important to know that there are defects and to understand their nature than to discuss and devise plans for remedying those defects. Yet the lecture sufficiently indicated the only basis of a plan that would give satisfaction, because justice, to all classes of citizens. In endorsing the views of John C. Spencer whose words were quoted, I said: "Whenever a time comes for the settlement of the school question upon an equitable basis, we shall have to go back to something like what John C. Spencer proposed in 1841." His words will bear repetition: " It is by adopting the principle of the organization that prevails in other parts of the State which shall leave such parents as desire to exercise any *control* over the *amount* and description of *religious instruction* which shall be given to their children the opportunity of doing so. This can be effected by depriving the present system in New York of its character of universality and exclusiveness, and by opening it to the action of smaller masses, whose interests and opinions may be consulted in their schools, so that *every denomination* may freely enjoy its *religious profession* in the education of its youth."

In other words John C. Spencer has placed education where it belongs—under the control of parents. There is no talk of church or church organization. A little attention to the meaning of words will show how senseless is the talk about *Church* and *State, State Religion,* etc. In countries in which all the people were of one religious belief the union of Church and State was possible, and they mutually aided each other. As the people changed their creed, or many fell off from the national religion, it took time to adapt the laws and government to the changed condition of religious belief and practice. All governments, Catholic and Protestant, made strenuous efforts to hold their subjects faithful to the established Church, to impede the introduction of the new form of worship, and to bring back the dissenters by the strong arm of power. In the monarchial or republican countries of Europe, the practical union of Church and State exists only by the slenderest thread and for the advantage of the latter. Even in countries whose inhabitants still, for the most part, profess the same creed, this union of Church and State is very weak, and day by day is giving way before the exactions and encroachments of civil rulers. With the lessons of modern history before us, and what is transpiring under our very eyes, how, I ask, is it possible to establish a union of Church and State in a country like ours, divided up into a hundred sects? or what is worse, having a majority of its population in the ranks of practical, if not avowed infidelity? It is not the possibility of union of Church and State which we have to dread. It is the tyranny of no-religion, of open infidelity, which, not content to have its own way, in the education of its own children, must compel every citizen, every parent, to accept the negative, defective, unchristian, infidel education for his children, which it, being in a majority, helped by the Evangelical churches, mercilessly imposes on its believing fellow citizens.

The danger now before us is in the threatened union of State and Infidelity, or union of State and Church of Infidelity. A Church is a body of people united in a common belief, and the Infidel Church is made up of all who believe in no-religion, no revealed truth, no rule of spiritual life to prepare for the world to come. This church is no phantom of the imagination ; it has its leaders, its organs of thought, its halls, its newspapers and literature ; it has life, activity, untiring energy, great aggressiveness ; its allies, found among professing Christians, as well as within its own fold, are the more dangerous, because concealed, and oftentimes, help the cause of infidelity without intending to stab Christianity to the heart. Among the allies of infidelity are all who bring discredit on the religion of Christ, by affecting indifference with regard to His explicit and positive teachings.

These good gentlemen of the infidel way of thinking seem to forget that any one has rights but themselves ; they are not satisfied to have " purely secular " education for their own children, they must, in a spirit of despotism incomprehensible in a free country, did we not know what strange things are done in the sacred name of liberty, labor to make other citizens, having equal rights with themselves, forego the dearest privilege of parents to educate their children with that *amount* and *description* of *religious instruction* which they may deem expedient. Mr. Abbott of Toledo, editor of the Index, a great light among the believers in no-belief, at a Convention in Syracuse in December last, spoke in this strain: " There is good in Christianity, but its fundamental idea—being founded on the will of Christ—is not consistent with liberty. It is enough to say to a Christian, ' It is the will of God or of Christ,' to satisfy him of a duty. But this is not sufficient." Exactly so. It is not sufficient for a child that does not believe in God, or in Christ ; but Christians do believe in God and in Christ as God, and they know no higher law than this will of God, nor do they care to form the consciences of their children on any other basis than that of loving submission to the will and law of God.

Parents have the natural and divine *right* to educate their children ; this right imposes a *duty* to provide for their offspring the best education they can. All educators of eminence speak of religious training as the chief part of a child's education, and agree in asserting that the teaching of morals is an essential part of the merest elementary education. Some, puzzled to know how to teach morals without religion, join the two, and say that all education ought to include morals and religion. We see how they embarass their cause by such admissions when they do not mean to be logical and consistent, and we vainly hope that common sense will lead them to take their stand with us. There is no midway in this problem of education. They must either teach their children morals and religion in such way, with such forms and by such instrumentalities as they possess, or throw over religion altogether, and substitute for it and God's law some such law as "Honesty is the best policy," or a selection of the eminently natural reasons for being a good boy furnished by Herbert Spencer and other writers of his class.

George Washington, whose name may possibly carry weight, even with those who reject the Bible, while they endorse Herbert Spencer, in his Farewell Address, makes use of this significant language: "Of all the dispositions and habits which lead to political prosperity, religion and morality are indispensable supports. In vain would that man claim the tribute of patriotism, who should labor to subvert these great pillars of human happiness, these firmest props of the duties of men and citizens. The mere politician equally with the pious man, ought to respect and cherish them. A volume could not trace all their connections with private and public felicity. Let it simply be asked, ' Where is the security for property, for reputation, for life, if the sense of religious obligation *desert* the oaths which are the instruments of investigation in the Courts of Justice?' And let us with caution indulge the supposition, that morality can be maintained without religion. Whatever may be conceded to the influence of refined education on minds of peculiar structure, reason and experience both forbid us to expect that national morality can prevail in exclusion of religious principles."

We might rest satisfied with these warning words of Washington, and adduce no other authorities to add to their weight, but, as the friends of the "Godless" schools admit the necessity of teaching morality provided it be divorced from religion, it is expedient still more to strengthen this position.

You cannot teach Christian morality without introducing religion. The Christian religion forms and directs the conscience. You cannot instruct a child in the Christian religion without telling it who Christ is, what He said and did, why He suffered and was put to death, nor can you read the simplest narrative of His life without provoking in your hearers the desire to ask questions. To say that the pupil shall not be permitted to ask questions, or the teacher to answer them, is manifestly absurd. With the asking and answering of questions concerning Christ, you introduce into the school the teaching of the Christian religion in some form, with such coloring, neutral or positive, as may be in the teacher's mind. The Rev. A. D. Mayo of Cincinnati, Unitarian Minister, presents this view of the case in the following strong and striking language: "It is easy to elaborate a 'secular' theory of education in the closet, where an ideal boy can be placed in a spiritual vacuum, and developed according to an exclusive mental system. * * * Now, the effort to control and educate such a miniature republic on 'secular' or purely intellectual principles is a job compared with which harnessing Niagara to turn the spindles of a cotton mill would be a cheerful enterprise. You have no place there to set up your fine machinery that shall isolate the intellectual power and handle it so delicately that the religious and moral susceptibilities may not be disturbed. You have no time there to demonstrate how much of a child is mind, how much is soul, and how much is animal. The clock strikes nine; and you are facing fifty full-blooded uproarious, Western boys, seething down from a mob to a school, and what do you propose to do with this tremendous fact? An American argus, with its hundred eyes, glares right into your face; pierces through your shams; pokes fun at your fine theories, and cries out, 'What do you want of me?' To say that the teacher does not need every resource of religious and moral power, save the ecclesiastical and theological, for which children care nothing, to govern and educate this community, is to mock at all educational experience and declare ourself utterly ignorant of human life."

The Rev. Doctor will not take it amiss if some children of a larger growth should happen to poke fun at his "fine mental theory" of religion, that is neither "ecclesiastical nor theological." Further on I shall have something to say of this new attempt to get around the difficulty of not divorcing morality from religion by divorcing religion from theology.

In sustainment of my proposition that religion cannot be eliminated from education, I will give the words of the "Democrat and Chronicle," of this city, in the ablest reply to my lecture that has come under my notice. In a carefully prepared article in its issue of December 23, 1871, it strives to answer the chief objection to the present Common School, and yet makes the following admissions: "There are at least three broadly divergent channels of thought, into which every thinker drifts, and which convey every teacher worthy the name. And while, in its highest aspect, the thought of the world may be above the comprehension of youth, and not required to be communicated to them in their early education; yet, on the other hand, so interwoven are all our relations, that it is impossible to avoid directing the youngest in one or the other of these channels, from the moment they first begin to think. The conception which the Romanist has of the universe, differs decidedly from that of the advanced Evangelical mind, as that in turn differs from the purely Scientific Religionist. How is a teacher to avoid coloring his instruction by the sentiments he cherishes? The theological idea

—that is, some view of the power which dominates in the universe—is inseparable from any intelligent educator's course of instruction. Yet in order to keep out the clashings and differences which agitate the purely theological world, we exact of our teachers that they shall do that which in the nature of things is impossible, if they are competent for the task,—hold convictions regarding the structure of the universe, and man's relations to it and its moving cause, and yet keep its rudimentary principles to himself while necessarily dwelling upon subjects inseparably connected with them. Of course there are some elementary branches —as arithmetic, grammar, etc., in the instruction of which no such difficulty presents itself; but the moment the student advances from these he engages in studies interwoven with the universe, and in their investigation he must necessarily follow one of the three forms of thought we have mentioned. And, what is more significant to Catholic and Protestant, is the fact that the more thoroughly a teacher succeeds in excluding all tincture of the theological idea, the more surely will he succeed in drifting into the third channel of thought which divides the thinking world; and hence it is that the Catholic holds our system to be 'Godless.' The same problem enters into the question of morals. We are apt to respond to the charge that our Common School system is 'Godless' in theory, at least, by saying that sound morality is inculcated. Yet the system of morals prevalent in the three schools of thought so widely diverge that they are irreconcilable; and, if we omit, as we practically do, the moral relations between man and his Maker, we again encounter the objection of the Catholics that our schools are 'Godless.' * * *
The position taken by Bishop McQuaid, that the Common School system is, in its theory, devoid of the religious idea, and in its tendency unsatisfactory to any religionist of every persuasion, we admit. The position, also, that the State ought not to undertake to educate children in antagonism to the faith of their parents, we also concede."

As we are contending for principles, and as the Democrat and Chronicle concedes substantially our main positions, we can afford to be indulgent over the harsh language with which the editor closes his article. The writer, who has a fine philosophical mind, should, however, consult Dr. Anderson upon the greater or less danger to the faith and morals of the very young, such as are found in our Common Schools. The Doctor will tell him that the tender and plastic mind receives impressions before it has knowledge and intelligence to repel dangerous and insidious teachings and suggestions; he will learn furthermore that a sneer, a cold look, a curl of the lip from an unbelieving instructor, may chill, if it do not kill, the simple and budding faith of the child; that a mother's anxious and loving care to instil into the mind and soul of her darling a spirit of love, trust and reverence may be rendered vain by the blight of indifference for sacred and religious things that falls upon a school from which God has been excluded, or in which He can be spoken of only in bated breath; nor will the Doctor forget to tell him that yet more subtle and insidious is the danger that arises from the *tone* of the school, such as prevails where the boys, ever ready to be a law to themselves, have ruled that it is unmanly, girlish, soft, to be religious, and that this danger is greater in young boys such as frequent our Common Schools, than it is in more advanced pupils whose intelligence and reason enable them to withstand human respect and false pride.

After clearly stating that all teaching will necessarily run in one of three channels—the Catholic, the Protestant or the Infidel—the writer with strange inconsistency and disregard of justice maintains that it shall run in the Protestant channel. It is true he only stands by the practice of the schools in Rochester which are to all intents and purposes Protestant schools. They are opened daily by the reading of the Protestant Bible, praying and religious singing; and this is done in direct contempt of the laws of the State of New York, which forbid religious exercises of any kind within school hours. The Democrat and Chronicle is surely able to perceive that the time is not far distant when, if no Catholic call for the observance of the law, there will be found others to demand the complete secularization of the schools as the law directs. According to the theory of the Democrat the channel of thought in religion and morals along which the pupils of our Common Schools will then be conveyed will be the Infidel one.

They have the "secular" system out West, and though the country is only in its infancy they are becoming annoyed at the young heathens which their schools are turning out. In the fifteenth biennial report of the Superintendent of Public Instruction to the General Assembly of Iowa, the Hon. A. S. Kissell discourses as follows: "The painful fact is, that the great mass of instruction now provided our youth—except perhaps the rambling and imperfect methods adopted in our Sabbath Schools—is a practical denial that any such value attaches to our national religion. We may listen all day to the exercises of any of our most efficient schools, and hear often enough excellent advice given to the pupils with reference to the importance of a generous, noble and virtuous character; we may be satisfied that the rules and discipline of the school are administered in such way as to secure habits of order, industry and good behavior; but we cannot help feeling that essentially the same feat might have been achieved in ancient Athens, as in our modern Boston, which stands so conspicuously as a representative city in Christendom. Somehow here, in this nursery of our nation, in the public schools, a perpetual libel is filed against the religion we adopt. Must these schools have no higher standard than refined heathenism could furnish?   *   *   *   Will it not be ill-timed and futile to urge upon the adult, that of which, during all the years of his early training, he heard nothing, and which was so effectually denied or ignored in the course of his training, that, but for the reputed Christian character of the teacher, and the devotional exercises with which his school was opened, he would not have known that the formation of his character had any conceivable dependence on such an influence."

The remedy for this lamentable condition of religious training in the schools of a Christian country is, according to the Hon. Mr. Kissell "To teach Christianity stripped of its theological amplifications," "Make the life and sayings of the Great Master the subject of formal historical study in the school-room," "Put the child in possession of the central fact of the Christian scheme."

I would like to see Mr. Kissell and the Rev. Mr. Mayo stand before a crowd of Western school boys and answer their questions about Christ and the Christian scheme without becoming "Theological," or even extending into "theological amplifications." Theology, I always thought, meant speaking about God. To avoid theology or theological instructions then, you must avoid speaking of God. I would like to hear Mr. Mayo explain the words of St. John, "In the beginning was the Word, and the Word was with God, and the Word was God. And the Word was made flesh," and not be "ecclesiastical or theological;" or even tell those boys what St. Paul meant by "One Lord, one faith, one baptism," or what Christ was thinking of when He gave the commission to His apostles which we find in the close of St. Matthew's Gospel, "Going, therefore, teach ye all nations: baptizing them in the name of the Father, and of the Son, and of the Holy Ghost: Teaching them to observe all things whatsoever I have commanded you: and behold I am with you all days, even to the consummation of the world."

Did Christ mean what he said? Have his commands and promises been kept? And if so, how and when? It would help the solution of this educational problem to hear either of these gentlemen give a straightforward and intelligible answer to these and other queries concerning Christ, His character, His office, His mission, His work, His death,—to such queries as might arise in the mind of any clever, bright Western boy, pondering over the sayings and doings narrated in the Gospels, and do so without trenching on ground "ecclesiastical or theological." Then if there is a morality without religion, or a religion without God, or that is neither ecclesiastical nor theological, and yet all sufficient for the young, why cannot these gentlemen tell us what it is, define it, make known its teachings, give its credentials, and introduce it among the parents of the children? It will soon supplant the thousand and one sects that remain "ecclesiastical and theological."

We have a right to ask the upholders of the present system of Common Schools to explain what is meant by State "Secular" education. Does it mean reading, writing and arithmetic? Does it propose to furnish its children with no more than the first and simplest tools of education to be used in opening the way to a higher standard? Or does the State undertake to provide educational facilities up to the highest point for all who may choose to make use of them? That this last is not a chimerical idea, but is working its way through the heads of the great army of school teachers, I will give a passage from a paper read by the Hon. Newton Bateman, of Illinois, at the National Educational Convention, held in St. Louis, in August, 1870: "The question for American statesmen is not how *little*, but how *much* can the State do for the education of her children; that the one thing most precious in the sight of God, and of good men, is the welfare and growth of the immortal mind, and that to do this, legislatures should go to the verge of their constitutional powers, courts to the limits of liberality of construction, and executives to the extremes of official prerogatives. I believe that an American State can and should supplant the district school with the high school, and the high school with the university, all at the public cost—exhibiting to the world the noblest privilege of the country—*a model free school system; totus teres atque rotundus.*"

Superintendent William Harris, at the same Convention, said: "The government of a republic must educate all its people, and it must educate them so far that they are able to educate *themselves* in a continued process of culture, extending through life. This implies the existence of *higher institutions of public education.*"

Similar utterances are heard from time to time in different parts of the country in Teachers' Institutes, and educational conventions. But facts are stronger than words. The common school has already its high school, its free academy, its normal school, its college of New York and its Cornell university,—the crowning glory of the system. So much has been accomplished in the last few years! What daring imagination will venture to picture the history of the next twenty years? We cannot stop and halt in the work. There is no reason now why the high school and free academy should not be found in every village and town of the State; there is no reason why normal schools should not cover the land;—they are so convenient for giving a superior education to many at the cost of the State;—there is no reason why there should not be a Cornell university in Buffalo, in Rochester, in Syracuse, in Schenectady, in Hamilton, in Canton, in Clinton, in Geneva, as well as in Ithaca. Let the State of New York, so mighty and so opulent, establish universities for the people everywhere, without regard to cost. So great a State cannot sit down to count pennies when it is a question of equal rights to all. The people want universities, as they have schools, "without sectarian bias," "that will be an antidote for bigotry and sectarianism;" "that will bring the children of all denominations together during the formative period of their lives." "Denominational schools (colleges and universities), are essentially narrowing in their tendencies and influence, upon the minds of youth. They encourage the very natural disposition in human society to divide into classes, while the common schools (colleges and universities), are peculiarly democratic. The latter foster toleration; the former encourage bigotry and clannishness and those who would increase their number at the expense of common schools are enemies of toleration. People who confine their children within the associations of their own church retard them in culture and contract their mental and moral powers. In after years they have to unlearn what has been industriously instilled into their minds by sincere but narrow minded instructors, if they ever become broadly sympathetic and charitably tolerant towards the many who will always think different from them."

Thus the arguments against denominational schools tell with equal force against denominational academies, colleges and universities. The people's children taught and trained in the common schools to despise all bigotry and "narrow-minded intolerance," reject as beneath their enlightened standard denominational colleges, and as they have a right to the highest education in the best institutions, they demand the establishment of Cornell universities all along the line, from Buffalo to New York. How long, I may be permitted to ask, will the Baptist, Methodist, Universalist, Presbyterian and Episcopal colleges survive the establishment by the State, with unlimited State funds, of rival and competing non-sectarian universities? Yet the right of the people to demand a full supply of non-sectarian colleges and universities, in view of the principles enunciated by the advocates of the common school system, cannot be questioned.

Why should the State hold its hand when the work is only half done? The college and university but lay the foundation for life's work. That work is found in the professions. It is important for the people to have sound lawyers and skillful and well instructed physicians and surgeons. Why should not the State furnish the very best schools of law and medicine, just as it proposes to found schools for the arts, sciences and trades? The State offers to be father to its children, and it ought to do its full duty to all.

In this arraignment of the State there is another neglect of duty still more serious for which it should be taken to task. The advocates of the common school system justify the action of the State in assuming to educate its children in public schools on the plea of economy. It is cheaper, they say, to build schools than poor-houses and prisons. Education makes a people moral, and a moral people will keep out of prisons and poor-houses. The same argument has equal weight in behalf of the establishment of institutions—churches, for helping people to remain moral and virtuous. The boy soon forgets his lesson, and the State that has undertaken to keep him out of prison and poor-house by making him moral must go on with its work and provide its ward with churches on a broad principle of morals and free from all "sectarian hate" and unpleasantness. It is true this work belongs to the denominations, but the denominations have failed to do their full work, and what they have done is not well done. They have not a sufficient number of churches; the expense attending them is too great for the poor; even the rich turn from them; they are "too narrow-minded and bigoted;" they hinder "the unification of the nation;" "encourage the very natural disposition in human society to divide into classes;" "retard culture and contract mental and moral powers."

Then, as a people must be moral to keep out of the poorhouse and the prison, why should not the State for its own welfare and in a spirit of economy found and support institutions—call them churches, if you please—for the instruction of the whole body of the people in morals and such rules of life as will help to keep them independent of State bounty and support, except in the matter of education and morals. Under this beneficent and paternal care the wards of the State will be provided with noble halls, and whilst orators of refinement and culture and the highest attainments are discoursing eloquently and pleasantly to them, the "bitterness of sectarian hate" will be seduously excluded. The Hon. Mr. Bateman, State Superintendent of Public Instruction in Illinois, says: "The discords, bitterness, antagonisms and dogmatisms of religious sects are the shame and scandal of Christendom, and a libel and burlesque upon the teachings of Christ, and the shame, scandal, libel and burlesque are only intensified by saying that these hideous things are inevitable among Christians." The national religion, without a creed, now about to be inaugurated with all the wealth of the State at command, will remove all these scandals from the churches as it has driven them out of the schools. Its religion, having in view only the moral welfare of its subjects,—its children will not be sectarian or denominational, but broad, liberal, "full of simplicity and love, including all the moral maxims and ethical principles that men deem valuable;" "it will exalt God, and holiness and truth only;" "it will have nothing to do with the devices of men;" under it "whoever loves truth and obeys Jesus Christ is an heir of heaven whether he has any human certificates to that effect or not." These are the arguments of the common school advocates by which they justify the secularization of education. Upon the introduction of this common, free, national religion, it is probable that denominational churches and institutions for the inculcating of moral truths under sectarian control will survive but a limited period of time. There may be some who will protest against this meddling and interference on the part of the State, but the ready supply of arguments used to defend the common school system will be at hand to justify the State in furnishing instruction for the people in the interests of morality, good citizenship, the unity of the nation and economy. Here is the language of one of the Apostles of the new creedless religion, Mr. Abbot of the *Index:* "In his mind's eye he saw the time when there should be no churches, but men would worship everywhere; but all should be brothers. There may be halls of culture and fixed ways to advance humanity, but they will need no church." What a choice but comprehensive expression. "Fixed ways to advance humanity." Of course, they will be fixed, very determined, very positive, very arbitrary. We have one of the "fixed ways to advance humanity" in the present common school system.

At the same convention at which Mr. Abbot foreshadowed the future national religion, the Rev. Mr. Towne gave a specimen of the manner in which he taught religion that was not sectarian to the inmates of the House of Correction at Detroit: "They do recognize a divinity in man—the Creator clothes the creature man with this divinity. It is said God descended into humanity through the Lord Jesus. Why not say it of all men? The true

Christ as sent to us from God, is in Nature. Wherever love is, there is the Christ also. The humane then is religion. Men may be religious according to their humanity." This is not sectarian, but is good, sound, State or National religion.

I am not straining my argument for effect.—Greater changes have flowed from smaller and weaker beginnings. The daily and untiring literary labors of armies of Commissioners, State and County Superintendents, teachers almost numberless, and hosts of others, working on the same line, with a united will and purpose, will not find it a herculean task to disseminate their ideas all over the country, and establish this " fixed way to advance humanity."

We are told that there shall be no change in the present system. But when we ask them to tell us what is this system, they are not able to agree among themselves. They cannot say if it is "education with religious instruction," or "education purely secular and without religious instruction of any kind."

In New York State the law reads that there shall be no religious exercises of any kind in any of the public schools of the State, outside of the city of New York, within school hours. If I have misunderstood or misstated the law, the Hon. Mr. Weaver, State Superintendent of Public Instruction, will, when consulted on the subject, correct the mistake. The practice in most of the schools, and notably here in Rochester,* is to ignore the law, and in utter disregard of the rights of a minority, for the majority is made up of Evangelicals, to have that amount of Bible reading, praying and the singing of hymns which seems pleasing to them.

Passing on to the State of Ohio, we discover that " our common schools cannot be secularized under the constitution of Ohio." " It is a serious question," says Judge Hagans, " whether as a matter of policy merely it would not be better that they were, rather than offend conscience;" and he then decided that the

---
* Since the above was written, Rochester has put Bible reading, prayer and religious exercises out of her schools.

resolutions of the Cincinnati Board of Education, forbidding religious instruction and the reading of religious books were "unconstitutional and void."

Journeying still further West, to Missouri, we find that the law and the practice are against religious instruction of any kind in that State. They are pushing secularism to its extreme limit.

Coming back to the Atlantic sea-board, in the little State of New Jersey, the public schools are conducted on the principle of imparting religious instruction that is thoroughly and essentially Protestant in character. Lest the Protestant teaching in the schools should not be sufficient, the State Superintendent of Public Instruction, whose salary is paid by Catholic and Protestant, is careful to furnish the school districts with lists of books for public school libraries containing the works of the most bitter anti-Popery authors.

No less discordant are the newspapers in their opinions on this question of religion in the schools. Thus, the Rochester Democrat and Chronicle holds that "it would be folly to sacrifice the Bible." The Rochester Express calls for secular education without sectarianism, but does not give its opinion of the practice of the Rochester schools to give religious instruction in contravention of the State law. The New York World favors as much religion in the schools as will give the pupil a salutary fear of the gallows and State prison: "It (the State) undertakes to give the child such knowledge as shall put him in the way of earning his living and shall make him afraid to get it by murder or robbery." "But he may be greedy, scheming, unscrupulous, and altogether objectionable as a human being. The State takes no account of that, but turns him over to the church to have his depravities chastened out of him." The New York Herald is in favor of having the Bible in the schools—is not particular about the version, and prefers that the reading should consist of only 'a short Psalm, a few Proverbs or something akin." The New York Tribune gives up the Bible as the only means of defending the Common School system with consistency. The Albany

Morning Express defends " secular " education free from any sectarian bias. " The occasional exceptions but prove the rule, which may, at any time it is infringed, be enforced by an appeal to the proper authorities." This means that the infringement of the rule forbidding religious exercises may be stopped here in Rochester whenever an appeal is made to the proper authorities. The Troy Daily Times, in an article most courteous and moderate, whilst strongly upholding the common school system, says : " We do not think that religious training is needful in the schools. * * * * The true function of the common school is to teach the rudiments of useful knowledge : to fit the child for acquiring the learning to meet the practical duties, which require a decent degree of intelligence and some technical knowledge." I am afraid the Troy Times will not advocate the establishment of additional Cornell universities at the public expense. The Utica Herald also sides with those who would remove the Bible from the schools.

When we leave the Press to come under the Pulpit the disagreement does not end. Ministers of religion are not of one mind on this vital question of religion or no religion in the common schools. There is no difference of opinion among them with regard to the education to be given to the sons of the wealthier classes who frequent academies, colleges, seminaries and universities. These are to receive a religious training in denominational institutions. Rev. Mr. Mann and Rev. Mr. Saxe of this city, and Rev. Mr. Spraeker of Albany speak out in favor of secular education without religious instruction or Bible reading. Other clergymen in this city and elsewhere are equally loud in calling for the reading of the Bible, prayer and the singing of hymns. The Rev. Dr. Clark of Albany, in a pamphlet that has obtained the endorsement and warm approval of the Rev. Dr. Wm. B. Sprague of Albany, of the Rev. Dr. Andrew P. Peabody, of Harvard College, of the Rev. Dr. Isaac Ferris, Chancellor of the New York University, and of the Hon. Ira Harris,

LL. D., late United States Senator and Chancellor of the Rochester University, gives the views of the evangelical denominations who constitute the more numerous body in the community, and who give tone and direction to the commom schools.

Rev. Dr. Clark and the others with him say: " Our fathers built this nation on the Bible. This sacred volume they placed in the family, the church and the school. They knew what every intelligent man knows, that the chief fact about any nation and its ruling power, is its religion.   *   *   * . The ignorance, the superstition, the temporal desolation, the spiritual fetters, the crimes, the wretchedness in these countries, (Italy, Spain and Mexico) are the outgrowth of Romanism. Our fathers desired to create on this soil a nation of which God would be the soul and center; the radiating point of influence that would shape our government, character, schools, families, literature, and mould the whole social and domestic condition of the people. They had the sagacity to see that their success in this work depended upon having the children and youth in the land educated as God would have them educated, in the principles and duties unfolded in His Holy Word. If we are to have a Christian nation, it must be by force of Christian ideas instilled into the hearts of the young.   *   *   *   It is clear from the history of the free school system of America that it had its origin in the desire to maintain the truths of the Bible in the hearts of all the people. The Bible is, in fact, its source.   *   *   *   To remove, therefore, the Bible and its sacred principles from our system of education, would be to take from that system its very soul, its life-giving power. How, then, can any one call the Bible, that reveals to us 'religion,' a sectarian book?   *   *   *   If it is opposed to Romanism, it is not because it is a Protestant book, but because it is God's book, the light of which, if permitted to shine, would sweep all the darkness, and errors, and iniquities of Romanism from the earth.   *   *   *   The Bible has never injured them (the Catholics) or their children. It damages Popery; it does not damage them. * * * It has been a matter of congratulation in years past, on the part of many Protestants, that so many Roman Catholics are coming to this country, that they might thereby be brought under evangelical influences; that we might, in the spirit of kindness and good-will, offer them a pure gospel; that seeing and experiencing the temporal blessing of a land filled with Bibles, they might be induced 'to search the Scriptures," and discover that the truths therein contained are profitable both for this life and the life to come." After quoting Rev. Mr. Mattison's statement that in twelve years one million nine hundred and ninety thousand Romanists had left the Catholic Church, he proseeds to say: "Of the correctness of this statement I have no means of determining; but this we do know, that multitudes have yielded to the influence of our institutions, and that *the most effectual agency in this work has been our admirable public school system.*

For the great medium through which *we* reach these classes with ideas and influences essential to qualify them to become good American citizens, is the public school system. We reach them through other instrumentalities—through our churches, Sabbath schools, and missionary enterprises; but our great hope in the work of enlightening, Christianizing, and Americanizing these masses, is through the system of public instruction founded by our fathers." "A school without the Bible educates them (the children) in the fatal fallacy that the State has nothing to do with religion. It leads them to infer that it is expedient and safe to have a school without a God, it is equally expedient and safe to have the family and society without a God."

We do not forget the words of the Rev. Nicholas Murray, Presbyterian clergyman, spoken at a May Anniversary meeting in New York, to the effect that whilst it was useless for them (the Protestants) to trouble themselves about the conversion of the adult emigrant Catholics, between the two stones of the mill, the Bible and the common schools, they would grind Catholicity out of their children.

How well satisfied they are with the working of the system, we may learn from the sermon of a Presbyterian divine of this city, preached on the 17th of December, 1871 : " Nay, there is a great deal of religion in our schools. Not in outward form, perhaps, but it is there. Our Saviour compared religion to salt; and salt in well cooked food does not so much lie in crystals on the surface or in lumps which you crush between your teeth, but is diffused through the whole man. And in our schools, from the ringing of the bell up to a recitation in the Anabasis, there is scarcely one thing that is not toned and shaped by the religion of our blessed Lord."

These extracts are long, but as they reflect the views of many of those who are opposed to us, it is right to give them. The spirit and motives of the evangelical party are brought out in plain language by the Rev. Dr. Clark. His words and suggestions coincide with the practice of the party represented by him, as the experience of Catholics tells us. Honest-minded men among our non-Catholic citizens will see that there is great cause for complaint of the injustice and wrong of the common school system, as it works against parents and citizens, whose views and feelings on religious subjects are not in harmony with those of the evangelical churches. We frankly confess that whilst very few of our children are drawn off to any of the evangelical churches, large numbers of them are weaned from their own religion and go to join the ever increasing ranks of unbelievers in any system of religion.

But our evangelical friends have taken a false position on this question which they are loath to quit. While they persist in attempting impossible things the battle is going on in favor of indifferentism and infidelity. As the combat thickens, the third party (the Catholic) quietly withdraws from the field, leaving evangelicalism to perish beneath the load of inconsistencies and fine philosophical theories which it chose to assume. There is hope that before the battle ends some of the evangelical denominations will see their mistake, discard false theories and go back to their original teachings and practices. Already the Baptist denomination, one of the most numerous in the country, is sounding the alarm. You have not forgotten the remarkable language of Dr. Anderson at a National Baptist Convention in New York city, in April, 1870. In May, 1871, the New England Baptist Educational Convention was held in Worcester, Mass. The work of that convention may be summed up in the resolution passed by the convention, recommending the establishment of at least one academy in each New England State for the education of children of the Baptist denomination. The necessity for these academies is found in " the defects of the public schools."

In the same month the Western Baptist Educational Convention met in Chicago. In the same sense and to the same purpose did the Reverend gentlemen speak in this convention.

The Convention of Southern Baptists, which met in Marion, Ala., on the 12th of April, 1871, having representatives from Virginia, South Carolina, Georgia, Alabama, Mississippi and Kentucky was even more decided and outspoken on the trouble in upholding the Baptist denomination. An address was delivered by Rev. Theo. Whitfield on the advantages of education in denominational colleges. In the course of the discussion which followed, the opinion was expressed by Dr. Poindexter, Professor Davis and Rev. E. B. League, that " the *tendency of the common school system was to foster infidelity,*" and that " *the only hope is Christian education in our own schools.*"

Whilst there is then great diversity of opinion among Legislators, Editors and Ministers respecting the imparting or withholding of religious instruction in the common schools there is yet another class who deny the right of the State to meddle in the education of children. Nor is this class insignificant in numbers or in influence. Furthermore, it is a class that from a variety of causes is daily growing in numbers and in influence. As the wealthier classes see the failure of the present system to embrace the great mass of the children, to bring about the promised economy, to diminish the number of paupers and criminals, they begin to ask, Has not a mistake been made? What right has the State to assume the duty of parents?

When such questions are being asked, does it not behoove the friends of the common school system to examine if some arrangement cannot be aimed at by which all can come under the working of the system in a way satisfactory to citizens of every class? Many who now attend private and religious schools, being deprived of their share of the taxes, will be compelled to join hands with the discontented wealth and capital of the country. This is not idle talk or foolish threat. You have only to step outside your own circle to learn that the elements of opposition are strong and growing. Every act of injustice, every day of injustice, adds to the strength of that opposition.

Rev. Mr. Mann tells us with great fairness that "it must be owned when we are told that in this city somewhere about one-third as many children are being educated in the Catholic schools as in the public schools, and that in so direct and costly a way almost the entire Catholic population repudiate the public school system, for the support of which they are taxed equally with others, it must be owned that the thing is not working justly. Facts like these are too significant to be overlooked. And as we inquire into the cause of such a state of things, the sense of its injustice deepens. It has ever been thought of questionable morality to tax for the support of the public schools a rich man who never patronizes them, preferring to keep a tutor in his own house; but we have got over that on the plea that *property* has an interest in education, and that the rich, for their own protection, must see that the poor are taught. But here is a large class who, in the main, are not rich, and who, from conscientious scruples of opinion, as they say, about religion, withdraw from the public schools, and do their part for the education of the poor in other institutions. When it is a rich man, who, for the sake of style, declines the benefit of the free school for his children, we say, justly enough perhaps, 'Let him go! Let him pay for his pride as dearly as he pleases!' But the case is somewhat different when the common people, from a sense of religious duty, mistaken or not as you please, pass by what they are compelled to pay for, and voluntarily pay over again to obtain the thing conscience requires."

The Hon. Gerrit Smith represents a large and increasing party, who maintain that governments should leave education alone. He says: "It (the government) is certainly no more fit to have a part in shaping and controlling the school than in shaping and controlling the church—and the sound arguments against its meddling with the church are, in the main, sound arguments against its meddling with the school. * * * No less is the parent's right to choose the kind of school than the kind of church for his children. Roman Catholics, and many Protestants also, are content with no school which is not positively and directly a religious one. Hence their opposition to the government school, which rests on an evil compromise—a compromise requiring the elimination from the school of all religion and use of all Bibles. * * * The government school has always, and necessarily, been a bundle of compromises; and now we are, but too probably, nearing the climax compromise of its divorcement from religion. Just here let me say that the school is far worse than worthless which, taking a child at its most plastic age, declines, nevertheless, to have a part in forming its religious character. * * * But we are told that one of the wise objects of the government schools is to prevent the getting up of sectarian schools. Our answer is, that it is no more the proper office of government to hinder the multiplying of sectarian schools than the multiplying of sectarian churches; and that the people are to be left as free to multiply the one as the other. * * * Government can never do more for its people than protect their persons and property. If thus protected they cannot prosper, then all the governments on earth cannot suffice to make the imbeciles prosper."

In the same sense and with equal explicitness did the late Rev. Dr. John C. Lord, Presbyterian Clergyman of Buffalo, in 1853, speak out on this subject: "Now the great objection which I have to the State Schools is, that they cannot teach religion. And, in my view, religious training should accompany all other teaching. God has not committed to Governments the work of education. The civil magistrate has other duties to perform; has no divine warrant to turn teacher or to superintend education. This is not a matter to be passed upon at the polls. Where the Church is united with the State she may derive some benefit from the State and allow the State to conduct her affairs. But in this country there is no union of Church and State. What right has the State to educate my child? The State may administer justice, build canals and railroads, incorporate banks, and perform civil functions, but it has no right to establish a system of public schools, which compels, in fact, the great mass of the community to have their children educated there or not at all. I wish my children educated 'in the nurture and admonition of the Lord,' and not in the nurture of the State. So do Christians in general, if the truth were known. But the State throws obstacles in the way by its taxation and its great public establishments."

The Rev. Dr. Lord being a consistent and earnest Presbyterian, followed the teaching of his church. The Presbyterians of America, at their General Assembly (1848), passed the following:

"Resolved, That this General Assembly, believing that the children of the church are a trust committed to the church by the Lord Jesus Christ, and having confidence in the power of Christian education to train them, with the divine blessing, 'in the way they should go,' do cordially recommend their congregations to establish primary and other schools, as far as may be practicable, on the plans sanctioned by the last Assembly— *of teaching the truths and duties of our holy religion in connection with the usual branches of secular learning.*"

Dr. Lord did not see how Presbyterians could hold to the teaching of his own church when the State usurped the work of imparting education "purely secular," without "religious exercises of any kind."

The Journal of Commerce of New York, in a series of articles, advocates the abandonment of the province of education by the State, and its relinquishment to the family and to religious and charitable zeal and effort, by arguments which the friends of the present system will find great difficulty in answering. Among other things, it says: "The issue, however, does not lie in the direction taken by the latter. It is probably between the school system as it is and its total abandonment, and the substitution of private instrumentalities, of course including church organizations, for State control. Our own preference of these alternatives has been more than once stated in these columns. But the agitation against the Bible and that in favor of introducing German, drawing, and other ornamental or professional branches of education into the common schools tend to hasten the conclusion we have advocated, namely; the abandonment of the work of education to private enterprise, charitable or otherwise, under such State supervision as may be necessary to prevent abuses."

These authorities are brought forward to prove that there are many who favor the total abolition of the present system of the State schools. Nor is their opposition based on whim or fancy; they have strong arguments to sustain their views, and it will not suffice to treat them with contempt.

Parents who are not pleased with state education because "purely secular," are politely requested to furnish schools and teachers for the instruction of their children after the ordinary school hours. They object to comply with this advice for several reasons. If they must furnish schools and teachers to do a part of the work, they may as well provide them to do the whole work. Sunday Schools are very good so far as they go, but they do not go far enough. Every one with his eyes open can see what efforts are needed to bring into the Sunday Schools the children even of the classes that have home instruction and require the Sunday School least of all; while the children whose homes are wanting in religious training and who do not obtain it in the state schools, are the ones most frequently absent from the Sunday Schools.

A serious and fatal objection to the proposition that the churches shall provide religious instruction for the children of the various denominations after school hours lies in the well-known law of human nature, that what becomes tiresome and annoying is not received with advantage. A child that has been restrained all day and kept at its books of secular learning will look with horror at the additional task imposed on its flagging and exhausted energies at the close of a hard day's work. We must not make religion distasteful to our children, even to please our friends of no-religion. Besides, an authority fully competent to speak on this question has decided that such a proposal cannot be entertained. The Medical College of Middlesex, Mass., has authorized the publication of the following facts as the opinions of its members:

I. No child should be allowed to attend school before the beginning of its sixth year.

II. The duration of daily attendance—including the time given to recess and physical exercises—should not exceed four and a half hours for the primary schools; five and a half for other schools.

III. There should be required no study out of school—unless at high school; and this should not exceed one hour.

The friends of the majority, wherever the law of New York state excluding the Bible, etc., is enforced, have a happy way of securing religious instruction for their children, without creating disgust by tacking on religious exercises after school hours, by having religious exercises before the opening of the classes, when the mind is fresh and vigorous. They admit our principle of the necessity of religious instruction for children, and secure its advantages for their own, in their own form of worship and belief, in school houses built by the taxes of all, and by the aid of teachers paid by general taxation. When the American people determine to recognize principles and equal rights for all, they will not be driven to expedients and subterfuges that are neither manly nor honest.

The Sunday school may be serviceable in supplementing the deficiencies of the week-day school, although it is well known that Sunday schools to prove attractive to the children that need them most, give a great deal of everything except religion. The good little boys and girls always go to Sunday school, but they are not the ones who threaten danger to our institutions, and whose future is a source of anxiety to all lovers of our country. The dangerous class is made up of boys and girls, full of life and vigor, whose homes are uninviting, with little of God and religion in them, who keep away from Church and Sunday school, and who, finding no religious instruction in the week-day school to form their conscience on the law of God, know only the law of the gallows and the State's prison.

The people are beginning to find out that the magnificent promises of the system are kept to the ear only. Already in our neighboring city of Buffalo, the Superintendent of education, in his annual report for 1870, complains of the preference manifested by parents for private schools: " The increase of the number and attendance of pupils at private schools, during the past ten years, is a subject for serious consideration. Formerly, the public schools monopolized almost entirely the education of our youth ; but, at the present time, private and religious schools are attended by nearly 25 per cent. of those who are of the school age. It is an interesting question, to ascertain the causes which have led to this diversion of pupils to other channels." It is more than an "interesting question "—it is a question of vital importance affecting the welfare of the state and the interests of the whole people. When these causes are ascertained, among them the chief one will be found to be that in Buffalo, one-half of its population agree with the late Rev. Dr. Lord that the State has no right to educate their children. Buffalo had in her public schools a daily average attendance of only eleven thousand children, whilst the whole number attending public, private and religious schools, according to the report of the Commissioner of Education, approached twenty thousand. If the diligent enquirer into the causes which are leading parents to prefer private and religious schools to those of the State will do us the favor of coming to Rochester, he will get some light on the subject when he learns that whilst the Commissioner of Education reports twelve thousand five hundred and eighty-six children in attendance in all the schools of this city, there are not many more than five thousand in daily average attendance in the public schools. We have four thousand and more in our Christian Free Schools; the balance may be found in the private schools of which, as I am informed, there are about fifty.

The annual report of the Board of Education of New York City for 1870, proves conclusively that, notwithstanding the enormous expenditures for the public schools, they have failed to win the confidence and patronage of the public. This report gives 109,554 as the average number on register for the grammar, primary, colored and corporate schools, and 92,355 as the average daily attendance. Yet the Commissioner of Education reports 155,603 as the number attending public, private and religious schools in New York City. To educate the 109,554 favored children the city paid $2,733,591.58. Yet it is well known that there are in the "Christian Free Schools" of that city over 20,000 children of the very class in whose favor the principle of State taxation for educational purposes finds its chief justification, whilst the number of children attending no other school than that of the street is as great to-day, relatively to the whole number of children in the city, as it was in the days of denominational schools as far back as 1805.

But to understand the full beauty of this system which thus punishes the parents of twenty thousand children for religion's sake, let us take a look at what is called the College of New York.

This college reports for the year ending June 30, 1870, seven hundred and ninety-six pupils, of whom four hundred and thirty-eight left or were dismissed for various reasons in the course of the year, and thirty were graduated. To give the three hundred and fifty-eight pupils who remained to the close of the scholastic year a suitable education there were required a President, with a salary of $4,750, a Vice-President, with a salary of $4,250, thirteen Professors, each having a salary of $3,750, a Librarian, receiving an equal amount, Tutors, Assistants and officers of various kinds, costing altogether for faculty and employes, $104,535.22.

Other payments increased the expense of educating these three hundred and fifty-eight pupils, in a grand palatial building already paid for, to $120,111.57. Yet because, for very shame's sake, a partial instalment of justice was dealt out to the schools in which the twenty thousand poor children were gathered, a howl is heard all over the land. We have learned, I hope, one great lesson from the past, namely to ask and demand justice and equal rights, and not favors or boons. Nor to dwell too long in the metropolis of the State, let us return to Rochester. If we have no "College of New York," we have a Free Academy and nineteen common schools, costing for the year ending March 27, 1871, one hundred and thirteen thousand three hundred and seventeen 56-100 dollars, to educate a few more than five thousand children. The Superintendent of Education in Rochester shows quite satisfactorily that here it costs only $13.58 for tuition per pupil in daily average attendance, whilst in Boston it costs $21.85, on the same basis, demonstrating conclusively how economical we are at the expense of our teachers, paying $400 in Rochester, where they pay $700 and $800 in Boston.

An illustration of the practical working of the system will bring it home to every taxpayer in the city. In the northwest corner of the town stands Public School house No. 17. On the corner of Saxton and Campbell streets, almost within the shadow of this school-house, lives a poor man, Jeremiah Callaghan, owner of a lot and small cottage, whose city tax for the present year was

$10.29, one-fifth of which (that being about the proportion of city taxes needed for the support of the city schools,) he paid for the education of his neighbors' children in No. 17, to which he did not send his own children, because he sent them to the Cathedral Free School. On Saxton street, not far from No. 17, lives Joseph Gradel, whose city tax bill amounted to $47.95, one-fifth of which went for the education of his neighbors' children in No. 17, to which he did not send his children, because he sent them to Saints Peter and Paul's Parochial school. On the west of No. 17 lives George Nunn, who paid $33, one-fifth of which went for the education of his neighbors' children in No. 17, to which he did not send his children, because he sent them to the Holy Family Parochial School.

If one of these children of Callaghan, Gradel or Nunn, in a fit of ill-temper, should tauntingly say to one of its companions of the neighborhood, "Oh, my father pays for your education, your father doesn't pay for mine!" could we accuse the child of untruthfulness, however much we might censure its want of politeness and amiability?

Any citizen of Rochester can take his city tax bill, divide the amount by five and thus learn how much he contributes directly towards the support of the Common Schools, whether he makes use of them or not.

When this question is fairly looked at and is brought home to every one; when the injustice of the present system, so opposed to all American notions of fair play and equal rights, is realized by the people, then may we hope for a change. The taxes paid by all will be enjoyed by all, no matter what a man's religion may be; it will not be possible to continue a system that favors one class in the community and works against another.

The Chicago Evening Post of December 26, 1871, heads an article "Hands Off!" and calls upon us "to let the public school system alone." It forgets, however, to tell the State to keep its hands out of our pockets. Unless we live under the veriest despotism ever known, the *right* to just and equitable taxation, and the *right* of all citizens to discuss the justice of that taxation has not been taken from us. No people are so sensitive to discussion as they who are conscious of wrong.

But besides those who oppose common schools on the grounds that governments have nothing to do with education and that the taxation is unjust, there is another party growing up and increasing in numbers, who assert that the public schools have failed to accomplish the work that was claimed for them. Nowhere in the United States has the system found greater development than in Boston. Its school houses are the largest and most expensive; its teachers, the best paid; its course of study, covering much and yet defective. If I were to sit in judgment on the common school system and point out its inherent defects my opinion would make little impression. With all due deference, therefore, to the invitation of a Presbyterian Minister of this city to visit and examine the schools of Rochester, I prefer to give the carefully prepared judgment of one whose standing in the country cannot be questioned. The Twenty-Seventh Annual meeting of the Massachusetts State Teachers' Association was held in Boston in October last. Professor Agassiz read a paper before this meeting, the first part of which paper we find condensed as follows in the Teachers' Journal of Boston: "We were too proud of our success, and too confident of the excellence of our school system. It had accomplished much but it had failed to give the people that culture necessary to the maintenance of republican institutions. * * * * Classes and schools were too large, and the teachers too few. The large school-houses reminded him of barracks for soldiers, rather than places where children are to be taught. Large schools demand a discipline which produces a uniformity which cramps and represses many scholars. * * * * The text-books are defective, and are mostly made by men who write as a trade rather than from knowledge." But if the Professor had reason to complain of the shortcomings of the public schools in these parts of the system, his cry of distress over the lamentable results of the moral training is heartrending. The substance of the second part of the Professor's paper is found embodied in an editorial article of the Boston Herald of October 20, 1871. "Year after year the Chief of Police publishes his statistics of prostitution in this city, but how few of the citizens bestow more than a passing thought upon the misery that they represent. Although these figures are large enough to make every lover of humanity hang his head with feelings of sorrow and shame at the picture, we are assured that they represent but a little, as it were, of the actual licentiousness that prevails among all classes of society. Within a few months, a gentleman (Prof. Agassiz) whose scientific attainments have made his name a household word in all lands, has personally investigated the subject, and the result has filled him with dismay, when he sees the depths of degradation to which men and women have fallen, he has almost lost faith in the boasted civilization of the nineteenth century. In the course of his inquiries he has visited both the well-known 'houses of pleasure' and the 'private establishments' scattered all over the city. He states that he has a list of both, with the street and number, the number of inmates, and many other facts that would perfectly astonish the people if made public. He freely conversed with the inmates, and the life histories that were revealed were sad indeed. To his utter surprise, a large proportion of the 'soiled doves' *traced their fall to influences that met them in the public schools*, and although Boston is justly proud of its schools, it would seem from his story that they need a thorough purification. In too many of them the most obscene and soul-polluting books and pictures circulate among both sexes. The very secrecy with which it is done throws an almost irresistible charm about it, and to such an extent has the evil gone that we fear a large proportion of both boys and girls possess some of the articles, which they kindly (?) lend each other. The natural results follow, and frequently the most debasing and revolting practices are indulged in. And the evil is not confined alone to Boston. Other cities suffer in the same way. It is but a few years since the second city in the Commonwealth was stirred almost to its foundations by the discovery of an association of boys and girls who were wont to indulge their passions in one of the school-houses of the city, and not long ago another somewhat similar affair was discovered by the authorities, but hushed up for fear of depopulating the schools. These facts demonstrate that parents and guardians do not do their whole duty by those committed to their care."

Only the other day it came out that in one of the public schools of Williamsburgh over one hundred vile and immoral publications were taken from the children frequenting that school.

Yet when parents and guardians wish "to do their whole duty by their children," and withdraw them from these "barracks" and the danger of such contamination, placing them in schools possessing their confidence, they are met by the pulpit and the press, and denounced in unmeasured terms as "sectarian," "narrow-minded and bigoted," "un-American," etc.

Just here some one may say to me that education, "purely secular," being an excellent antidote against crime, is all that the State requires in her function of preserving the peace and protecting persons and property. Indeed, the friends of the common school system manifest great anxiety to convince the world that this description of education lessens crime, and they arrange figures to prove their assertion, much to their own satisfaction. They all overlook the important fact that there are crimes, not merely speculative, or simply irreligious, that corrode and destroy human life and society, of which the criminal laws take no cognizance, and which do not enter into the tables of the statisticians. I might here enumerate many such crimes of whose frequency we are daily reminded by the press.

To prove that "education without religion" or purely secular does not keep men from even the crimes punished by the State, I will give you some strong and trustworthy authorities. John Falk, founder of the first House of Reform for juvenile offenders, said: "Of what use or advantage to the Commonwealth are rogues that know how to read, to write or to cypher? They are only the more dangerous. The acquirements mechanically imparted to such men, can serve only as so many master keys put into their hands to break into the sanctuary of humanity."

Ex-Mayor Bigelow of Boston, on a public occasion, said: "At the rate with which violence and crime have recently increased, our jails, like our alms-houses, will scarcely be adequate to the imperious requirements of society." Ex-Governor Clifford, in a letter to a gentleman of West Newton, Mass., used the following remarkable language: " I have a general impression derived from a long familiarity with the prosecution of crime, both as Attorney General and District Attorney, that the merely intellectual education of our schools in the absence of that moral culture and discipline, which in my judgment ought to be an essential part of every system of school education, furnishes but a feeble barrier to the assaults of temptation and the prevalence of crime; indeed, without this sanctifying element, I am by no means certain that the mere cultivation of intellect does not increase the exposure of crime by enlarging the sphere of man's capacity to minister, through its agency, to his sensual and corrupt desires. I can safely say, as a general inference drawn from my own somewhat extensive observation of crimes and criminals, that as flagrant cases and as depraved characters have been exhibited amongst a class of persons who have enjoyed the ordinary elementary instruction of our New England Schools, and, in some instances, of the higher institutions of learning, as could be found by the most diligent investigation among the convicts of Norfolk Island or of Botany Bay."

No later than the 28th of February, 1872, the New York Evening Post gives its testimony on this subject in the following words:

" It is a popular theory that ignorance is the parent of crime. That there is a fallacy in this is, however, proved by some figures presented in the report of the Inspectors of the State Penitentiary in Western Pennsylvania. Of the four hundred and eighteen inmates of this institution there are only forty-seven who can neither read nor write, and forty-four who can read only, while those who can both read and write number three hundred and twenty-seven. That is to say the proportion of illiterates among these prisoners is actually considerably less than the proportion of them among the whole adult population of the Northern States taken together. The same seems to be true of the other prisons. The reports from Auburn Prison, in this State, and from the prison at Columbus, Ohio, also show that the vast majority of criminals have received a fair education. The difficulty seems to lie in a misunderstanding of the term 'education.' It is construed to mean the mere elements of intellectual instruction without regard to home influences and moral training."

And if we examine every jail, penitentiary and prison, from the Atlantic to the Pacific, we shall not find one inmate that did not know that the crime for which he was incarcerated was punishable by the laws of the State, and that if caught and convicted he would be made to suffer the prescribed penalty of the law. Yet having expelled God, the Bible, prayer and religious exercises of any kind from the common schools, or keeping them in the schools in violation of the law, the training of our children is brought down to the "purely secular," or intellectual standard, spiced with a salutary fear of the gallows and the State's prison.

These are ugly truths, but they do not cease to exist because we try to shut our eyes to their existence.

After all this fault finding with the common school system, you have the right to ask, What can you propose as a substitute?

Strictly speaking, it is not the office of a Republic to meddle in educational matters. One of the chief merits of a Republic is that it leaves the people to govern themselves, so that they do not interfere one with another. That government is the best which governs the least. Under such an arrangement the people would take education into their own hands, and it would be better looked after, and at less cost. To say that republicans will not avail themselves of the advantages of education only as a charity is a libel on republicanism ; and when we see one hundred thousand children of the poorest class of the community educated by their parents, who at the same time pay taxes for the education of their neighbors' children, the charge is a calumny.

But the plan of State aid for education is so generally acceptable that no change need be looked for. My own preference is strongly in favor of having the State continue to aid educational institutions, provided it can do so with justice to all parties—with favor to none.

A plan that would least of all disturb the present system has been proposed by Elihu H. Shepard of St. Louis. In a communication to the Missouri Republican, February 22, 1872, he says: " I have mentioned in one of the foregoing chapters of this work the interest and active part I took in the establishment of the public schools of the city. It has placed St. Louis in advance of any city in the world for facilities for acquiring a good education. It has stimulated the opening of large, well-managed parochial schools in all parts of the city by different societies, which are building, or have built, magnificent edifices for educational purposes, and filling them with the most profound and able teachers of their respective societies for the instruction of their younger members, according to their own tastes and desires. Their success has been very remarkable, for it has been done without one dollar's aid from the public treasury, while every taxable member of these societies has been contributing to the support of the St. Louis public schools without much complaint. The time has now come for a small, and I think a very just and necessary change, and I intend to advocate it with the same pertinacity I did the school tax from its commencement to the present time, and will continue. A legislative act will be necessary to make the change, and it can be accomplished with almost imperceptible action, but with most easy and praiseworthy justice and entire satisfaction. The board of directors of the St. Louis public schools is already an incorporated body and is well known as such. Each society that has a literary edifice erected and has been in operation one public school scholastic year, can become incorporated and thereby enabled to ask and receive from the county treasurer such sum as has been paid in as public school tax by members of that particular society and placed to its credit by the person paying the tax and making his wishes known.

"Should action on this subject be much longer delayed, while we see such crowds flocking to parochial schools of different denominations, we may expect to see a combined oppositior formed against the present taxation that will endanger the labors of so many years."

Although the plan of Mr. Shepard is open to some objections, it would satisfy those persons who sneeringly tell us Catholics that our share of the taxes is so small that we are dependent on the charity of others; it would also quiet those other citizens who fear lest any of their money should be used for the support of "Popery." Whenever it is arranged to give us back the money paid by us for the support of schools, we will accept it as a just settlement, build school-houses for our children and educate them without troubling the State or our fellow-citizens. To be told to go about our business and not grumble, when our money is taken from us for the education of our neighbors' children, is too much for poor human nature. As we have never heard any one say that under similar circumstances he would feel happy, it is not surprising that we are somewhat miserable.

I would respectfully submit that the State continue to aid in the education of its children, define and describe the amount of education it is disposed to pay for, specify the conditions under which it will pay for that education, determine the annual sum *per capita* to be paid for it, and then pay that amount for that education wherever it finds it under the conditions imposed, whether it be in a large school or a small one, private or public, religious or purely secular.

State education will necessarily be restricted. There is no good reason why it should include more than the elementary branches of an English education, namely, Reading, Writing, Arithmetic, Geography and the History of the United States. When you pass beyond this limit the field is boundless; you cannot stop short of a University education. Under this plan the State will have dealings with the people—its citizens. It will be for them to say if they will have religion—the higher branches —a classical course—the refinements of a polished education in the schools to which they send their children. If they want more than the State agrees to pay for, let them pay what additional sum they please for their religion and accomplishments. The State will take cognizance of what it pays for and nothing else.

Many silly things have been said in reference to the agitation of this question. To listen to some people one would suppose the right of "Free Speech" had come to an end; that a public question in which all are interested should not be discussed; that the right of arbitrary taxation alone remained in a Republic the essence of whose life is the will of the people, founded in law and justice; that our young Nation which cast off its swaddling-clothes so quickly and so completely, is already as hide-bound by a system, because it is a system, as any old, shriveled up European despotism that has been growing with its pet systems for centuries past.

We have been invited to leave the country; there have been fearful mutterings of bloodshedding and war to the knife. Yet no one has been hurt, if some people's folly has been exposed. There is talk, they tell us, of a "No-Popery" party. Well, we have seen "No-Popery" times, the Native American party and the Know-Nothing party. We have passed through all these crucibles. Can any one point out in what way, in any degree, the Catholic Church has been injured by any or all of these outbreaks of insensate bigotry? The commotions but serve to call attention to the claims of the Church, induce thinking men to inquire into the nature of these claims, and end by giving the Church large harvests of earnest and sincere converts.

· We propose, with God's help, to continue this discussion—this agitation. We hope in time to enlist in it the sympathy and labors of many. It presents a fine field for the talents and abilities of our young men. In its study they will instruct themselves and learn how to instruct others. It is the work of the coming years. All other questions pale before it. If we are not to educate our children in our own faith, churches of more perishable material would be in order; these solid structures in brick and stone, arising on every side, would only stand as monuments of the folly of a race that so dealt in material things that it could not preserve for a few generations a faith handed down to it by persecuted ancestors who had treasured it lovingly and steadfastly in thatched chapels during centuries of hardship and martyrdom. Build school-houses then for the religious training of your children as the best protest against a system of education from which religion has been excluded by law.

Every consideration—every principle of American love of liberty and fair-play, calls upon us to resort to all legitimate and well-known means of influencing and changing the public mind. Our American friends and neighbors would despise us and hold us as unworthy the blessings of self-government, if with all the lessons of the past before us, we did not make use of these means to help our cause. We have the press, the rostrum and the newspaper. Our documents must be circulated by the hundred thousand; they must reach all classes in the community. The present system could not go on a year if the people fully understood all its workings and saw without prejudice the injustice inflicted on large classes of citizens. When the parents of the five thousand children attending the common schools of Rochester come to realize the fact that their children are receiving their education at the expense of their neighbors, whose children are educated in other schools; that these neighbors are poor men and poor women, in the same walk of life as themselves, struggling day by day to earn a moderate living, shame and proper self-respect will cause them to be unwilling recipients of what has the look of a charity, and a charity at the expense of their mates and companions in the shop, the store, the factory and the field. This spirit of self-respect, so strong in all Americans joined to their innate love of fair-play and equal rights, will cheer us on in our work of diffusing a knowledge of all sides of the question among our fellow-citizens.

I believe that many are held back from helping up through a dread that Catholics are not, for some cause or other, whole-souled Americans, and that some allegiance to a foreign power stands in our way of becoming identified with the country and its institutions. We know how false and unfounded is this accusation and we must labor to disprove it.

It is hard, I admit, to be called on to do this when we can point to such a record as we have already made in the country. George Bancroft bears this testimony to our beginnings in Maryland: "Under the mild institutions and munificence of Baltimore, the dreary wilderness soon bloomed with the swarming life and activity of prosperous settlements; the Roman Catholics, who were opposed to the laws of England, were sure to find a peaceful asylum in the quiet harbors of the Chesapeake; and there too, *Protestants were sheltered against Protestant intolerance.*

At the close of the war of the Revolution, George Washington, having received a letter of congratulation from Catholic citizens, wrote in reply: "I hope ever to see America among the foremost nations an example of justice and liberalty, and I presume that your fellow-citizens will not forget the patriotic part which you took in the accomplishment of their revolution and the establishment of your government or the important assistance which they received from a nation in which the Roman Catholic faith is professed."

In the war of 1812, and in the late war to preserve the Union, Catholics did their full duty side by side with their fellow-citizens. When soldiers were wanted to fight for the country, men did not stop to inquire if they were sectarian or Catholic, but if they loved their country and were ready to die in defence of its liberties. Our strongest and boldest advocates will yet be found outside our own body, and they would soon show themselves but for our own supineness and lethargy.

The positions taken by me in this and the preceding lecture may be summed up:

Parents have the right to educate their children.

It is wrong for the State to interfere with the exercise of this right.

By the establishment of Common Schools at the expense of all tax-payers, the State does interfere with this right, especially in the case of poor parents who find it a burden to pay double taxes.

It is for parents and not for the State to say how much or how little religious instruction they wish their children to receive.

The channel of thought in the Common Schools of this State is either the Protestant or the "Godless."

Wealthy Protestants educate their children in denominational academies, seminaries and colleges.

Common Schools are losing favor with the people who prefer private and religious schools.

Education "purely secular," or without religious instruction, does not lessen crime.

Large schools—"barracks"—especially without religious safeguards, are more than dangerous.

The State should limit the education which it is willing to pay for to the elementary branches of an ordinary English education, say what such an education is worth, and then pay for it, whenever it finds it under proper conditions.

The State will have nothing to do with churches, but only with parents and schools.

The discussion is a legitimate one for American citizens in a country of free speech, and no one needs to lose his temper.

It is absurd to discuss the question of intolerance abroad while we have such a glaring instance of intolerance at home.

No permanent *settlement* of this question is possible but one that recognizes the *equal rights* of *all citizens*.

We may trouble the politicians by our agitation. So much the better. It will give them a subject to exercise their ingenuity on worthy of their time and talents. Europeans come here to study our educational institutions. Let us have it in our power to show them a system of schools that embraces all the people, while sacredly guarding the heaven-born right of parents to control the instruction and training of their offspring. We shall have but sorry work to show them, if we can do no more than point out weak imitations of imported systems—systems so defective and unjust that over one-half the children of a town seek in private and religious schools, without the supervision of the State, an education in harmony with the views and feelings of their parents.

THE
PUBLIC SCHOOL QUESTION

AS UNDERSTOOD BY A CATHOLIC AMERICAN CITIZEN.

A LECTURE

DELIVERED BY

B. J. McQUAID,

BISHOP OF ROCHESTER,

BEFORE THE FREE RELIGIOUS ASSOCIATION (FREE THINKERS) OF BOSTON, AND AT THEIR REQUEST, IN HORTICULTURAL HALL, ON SUNDAY AFTERNOON, FEBRUARY 13, 1876.

LECTURE.

I WISH to say that I am here as a Catholic American citizen, speaking only for myself and my country, and in no way responsible for Mexico, South America, Spain, or any other country in the world.

The school question is engrossing more and more the attention of all classes in the country. Pres. Grant devotes a portion of his annual message to the subject, and calls for yet larger consideration of it by the legislatures of the States. Politicians worry and fret over it, not knowing how the current may chance to run, and consequently which course they should take. Ministers and editors, from pulpit and press, flood the country with their learning and wisdom, well spiced with warnings and threats to all who dare differ from them. And yet the last to be heard and consulted is the one to whom the settlement of the question first and finally belongs,—the parent of the child.

THE SCHOOL QUESTION TO BE SETTLED BY PARENTS.

The father may listen to well-meant good advice; his fears may be excited by denunciations of impending peril for himself and offspring; laws may be enacted to interfere with his natural rights; he may be mulcted through his purse, and harassed in many ways; his neighbors may turn against him:—yet, in despite of all, the responsibility of the education of his child falls on him, and on no one else. He may be assisted in his work by others, if so he will, but in accordance with his will and choice, and not according to the conscience of his neighbors or of his fellow-citizens.

PARENTAL RIGHTS BEFORE STATE RIGHTS.

Parental rights precede State rights. Indeed, as the Declaration of Independence has it, governments are instituted to secure man's inalienable rights; and among these are life, liberty, and the pursuit of happiness. A father's right to the pursuit of happiness extends to that of his children as well. This happiness is not restricted to material and earthly enjoyment, but reaches to every thing conducive to joy, pleasure, contentment of mind and soul, in this world and the next, if the father believes in a future life.

PARENTAL RIGHTS AND DUTIES ACCORDING TO COMMON LAW.

Parental rights include parental duties and responsibilities before God and society. The common law is explicit on this point, as Blackstone and Kent assert, "A parent may, under circumstances, be indicted at common law for not supplying an infant child with necessaries." (Chitty on Blackstone.)
"During the minority of a child .... the parent is absolutely bound to provide reasonably for his maintenance and education; and he may be sued for necessaries furnished, and schooling given, to a child under just and reasonable circumstances." (Kent's Com., Vol. II., p. iv.; lec. xxix.)

THE COMMON LAW DEFINED BY JUDGE LEWIS.

The rights of parents are strongly and clearly defined by Judge Ellis Lewis, in "Commonwealth v. Armstrong, Lycoming County, Penn., August session, 1842." The judge, having sent his decision to Chancellor Kent, received in reply an approval of its correctness, and of the reasoning on which it was based. In this opinion Judge Lewis says, "The authority of the father results from his duties. He is charged with the duty of maintenance and education .... The term 'education' is not limited to the ordinary instruction of the child in the pursuits of literature: it comprehends a proper attention to the moral and religious sentiments of the child. In the discharge of this duty, it is the undoubted right of the father to designate such teachers either in morals, religion, or literature, as he shall deem best calculated to give correct instruction to his child." In sustainment of his opinion, the judge quotes from Horry, professor of moral philosophy, from Dr. Adam Clark, from Paley, and from Dr. Wayland, who in his Moral Philosophy writes, "The right of the parent is to command: the duty of the child is to obey .... The relation is established by our Creator.... The duty of parents is to educate their children in such a manner as they (the parents) believe will be most for their future happiness, both temporal and eternal.... With his duty in this respect, no one has a right to interfere.... While he exercises his parental duties within their prescribed limits, he is, by the law of God, exempt from interference both from individuals and from society." After citing these authorities and various passages of the Sacred Scriptures, the judge goes on to say, "It is the duty of the parent to regulate the conscience of the child by proper attention to its education; and there is no security for the offspring during the tender years of its minority, but in obedience to the authority of its parents in all things not injurious to its health or morals."

BY THE SUPREME COURT OF WISCONSIN.

The Supreme Court of Wisconsin, in 1874, went so far in maintenance of parental rights, that it gave to a father the right to decide for his son what branches of elementary studies embraced in the school curriculum he should not follow against the will and decision of the teacher and the school committee. The court based its judgment on these indefeasible parental rights embodied in the common law.

DOES THE CHILD BELONG TO THE STATE?

It is the Christian view of parental rights and duties which is here given. It is presented under the supposition, that, however great in these United States the diminution of Christians in point of numbers, there may be left enough to constitute an important part of the population, with rights warranted by the natural, the divine, and the common law, worthy of consideration. The doctrine coming into vogue, that the child belongs to the state, is the dressing-up of an old skeleton of Spartan Paganism, with its hideousness dimly disguised by a thin cloaking of Christian morality. The most despotic governments of Europe illustrate the fruits of the doctrine, by making every one of their subjects an armed soldier, for the butchering of fellow creatures in neighboring states, under the forms of legalized warfare.

THE EVANGELICAL CHRISTIAN'S AUTHORITY FOR PARENTAL DUTIES.

The evangelical Christian who believes in the revealed word of God reads in the sacred book the teachings of his Master on the respective duties of parent and child, and regards these teachings as the law of his life :—

"Children, obey your parents in the Lord ; for this is just.

"Honor thy father and thy mother; which is the first commandment with a promise.

"That it may be well with thee, and thou mayst be long-lived on earth.

"And you, fathers, provoke not your children to anger ; but bring them up in the discipline and correction of the Lord."—EPH. vi. 1-4.

"Children, obey your parents in all things ; for this is well-pleasing to the Lord."—COL. iii. 20.

THE CATHOLIC CHRISTIAN'S AUTHORITY.

The Catholic Christian, taught to hear the church which is commissioned to teach all divine truths with infallible certainty, learns that he cannot neglect the care and education of his children without grievous sin ; that their religious instruction demands his chief thought ; and that to expose them to danger in faith or morals, in schools or elsewhere, would bring on him the just anger of God, and punishment hereafter. He knows that an education which excludes God, and is confined to material thoughts and interests, is one of which for his children he cannot approve.

HOW THE CATHOLIC CONSCIENCE IS FORMED.

On the natural law, and on the law divinely revealed and presented to him by God's chosen agent, the Church, the

Catholic forms his conscience. He does not expect that his conscientious convictions in matters of religion will please others; no more is he pleased with the professed creeds of the majority of his fellow-citizens. These form their conscience on grounds satisfactory to them; he forms his on grounds still more satisfactory to him. "The divine law," says Newman, "is the rule of ethical truth, the standard of right and wrong; a sovereign, irreversible, absolute authority in the presence of men and angels." "The divine law," says Cardinal Gousset, "is the supreme rule of actions. Our thoughts, desires, words, acts, all that man is, is subject to the domain of the law of God; and this law is the rule of our conduct by means of our conscience. Hence it is never lawful to go against our conscience."

"Conscience," says Newman, "is not a long-sighted selfishness, nor a desire to be consistent with one's self; but it is a messenger from Him who, in nature and in grace, speaks to us behind a veil, and teaches and rules us by his representatives. Conscience is the aboriginal vicar of Christ, a prophet in its informations, a monarch in its peremptoriness, a priest in its blessings and anathemas; and even though the eternal priesthood throughout the Church could cease to be, in it the sacerdotal principle would remain and would have sway."

The theory of freedom of conscience guaranteed by the Constitution as a right is conceded to the Catholic by secularist and evangelical. The wording of the Constitution, and our loud boasting at home and abroad of liberty of conscience as a special privilege of democratic government, demand this concession. Theory and practice clash. The Constitution rules that all shall be free to follow the dictates of conscience, provided there is no encroachment on the freedom of others. The majority of the people rule, by the power of numbers, that a large majority shall not be free to educate their children according to their conscience.

THE CATHOLIC CONSCIENCE SHOULD BE FREE.

Having proved that the Catholic conscience is founded on the natural and the revealed law, protected in its right by the common law and the Constitution of the United States, the claim that Catholic parents should be untrammelled in the exercise of parental duties brings me to the consideration of school education as affecting this conscience.

It is conceded by free religionists, by the ablest of the secular press, by many representative ministers of the evangelical churches, and by large numbers of the people, that to tax Catholics, Jews, and Infidels for schools in which the Bible is read and religious exercises are held, is a wrong, an act of injustice, a form of tyranny. So, understanding the case, the cities of Troy, Rochester, Cincinnati, and Chicago, have forbidden religious exercises of any description in their common schools. This is a confession that would not have been made thirty years ago. It is a partial reparation of the past. Especially is it a warning to boards of education in other places to cease inflicting this mode of religious persecution on citizens who object to any kind of religion, or to the peculiar kind prevailing in their schools. Mr. Beecher says, " It is not right or fair to tax Catholics or Jews for the support of schools in which the Bible is read." His congregation applauded the saying. If it is not right, it is wrong, and Catholics who are thus taxed are, to the extent of the taxes they pay, punished—persecuted for religion's sake.

INFRINGEMENT OF CONSCIENCE IS PERSECUTION.

Judge Taft, in giving his opinion in the Superior Court of Cincinnati, in the case of Minor *et al. vs.* Board of Education of Cincinnati, expressed his judgment as follows : " We have this unequivocal evidence of the reality of their conscientious scruples, that when they have paid the school tax, which is not a light one, they give up the privilege of sending their children, rather than that they should be educated in what they hold to be, and what without the adoption of one or both of these resolutions must be fairly held to be, *Protestant* schools. This is too large a circumstance to be covered up by the Latin phrase, *de minimis non curat lex*, to which resort is sometimes had. These Catholics are constrained every year to yield to others their right to one-third of

the school money, a sum of money averaging not less than
$200,000 every year, on conscientious grounds. That is to say,
these people are *punished* every year for believing as they do, to
the extent of $200,000; and to that extent those of us who send
our children to these excellent common schools become beneficia-
ries of the Catholic money. We pay for our privileges so much
less than they actually cost."

I quote this distinguished authority to justify the exceed-
ingly strong accusation made a moment ago.

THE STATE HAS NO RIGHT TO EDUCATE.

The Catholic, however, is equally unwilling to transfer the
responsibility of the education of his children to the State. His
conscience informs him that the State is an incompetent agent to
fulfil his parental duties. While the whisperings of his conscience
are clear and unmistakable in their dictates, it pleases him to
hear what others, non-Catholics, have to say on this important
aspect of the subject.

The late Gerrit Smith, whose character as an able and fear-
less philanthropist I need not dwell on, in a letter of Nov. 5, 1873,
to Charles Stebbins of Cazenovia, and intended for publication,
says, " The meddling of the State with the school is an imperti-
nence little less than its meddling with the Church. A lawyer,
than whom there is not an abler in the land, and who is as eminent for integrity as for ability, writes me, ' I am against the
Governments being permitted to do any thing which can be
intrusted to individuals under the equal regulation of general
laws.' But how emphatically should the school be held to be the
concern and care of individuals instead of the Government! It
is not extravagant to say that Government is no more entitled to
a voice in the school than in the Church. Both are, or ought to
be, religious institutions ; and in the one important respect that
the average scholar is of a more plastic and docile age than the
average attendant on the Church, the school has greatly the
advantage of the Church."

The views of Gerrit Smith and of the Catholic parent coincide in a remarkable degree.

HERBERT SPENCER ON THE SAME SUBJECT.

Another authority will, I trust, be equally acceptable to my hearers. Herbert Spencer, in the chapter on National Education in "Social Statics," thus writes: "In the same way that our definition of State duty forbids the State to administer religion or charity, so likewise does it forbid the State to administer education. Inasmuch as the taking away by Government, of more of a man's property than is needful for maintaining his rights, is an infringement and therefore a reversal of the Government's function toward him, and inasmuch as the taking away of his property to educate his own or other people's children is not needful for the maintaining of his rights; the taking away of his property is wrong." Mr. Spencer then goes on to prove his proposition, and refute objections brought against it by various classes of objectors, thus: "The reasoning which is held to establish the right to intellectual food will equally well establish the right to material food; nay, will do more,—will prove that children should be altogether cared for by the Government. For if the benefit, importance, or necessity of education be assigned as a sufficient reason why government should educate, then may the benefit, importance, or necessity of food, clothing, shelter, and warmth be assigned as a sufficient reason why Government should administer them also. So that the alleged right cannot be established without annulling all parental authority whatever." The destruction of parental authority, and the uselessness of mere intellectual education as a preventive of crime, are the chief points he makes against State interference with schools.

THE JOURNAL OF COMMERCE ON THE SAME.

"The only remedy," says the "Journal of Commerce" of New York, "we see in the future for the evils which are admitted, is to be found in the entire separation of the educational process from State authority. If this has been found wisest and best in matters of religion, why not in relation to all forms of education? Youth needs the higher sanction of religion in every department of culture; and this cannot be secured in a State school where there is no State church."

It can scarcely be said that the interference or non-interference of the State in school education is an open question. By concession on the part of the large majority of the population, liberty to interfere is granted. This liberty in no way includes the right so to take part in the education of children that the just and inalienable rights of parents shall be sacrificed. I have dwelt on the argument of parental rights because the assumption of the State to control education, and the indifference of many parents to this assumption, encourage the supposition that all the right is in the State, and none in the parent.

COMMON SCHOOLS BEGAN ON A RELIGIOUS BASIS.

In the gradual establishment of State schools, the element of religious instruction always had a place of honor. The Constitutions of your New England States, and in a very remarkable degree those of Massachusetts and Connecticut, recognize God, religion, virtue, and morality. The departure of modern methods has been from the old and sound ways of the founders of the Republic, both as respects the religious element in the education of the young, and the duty of parents to bear the burden of their children's education. The Western States copied the Constitutions of the older States, and, like them, included morality and religion as essential parts of a sound education; but, falling into the prevailing error, learned to exclude God and religious instruction from their schools.

HAS EDUCATION YET DECREASED CRIME?

Now, hear their piteous lamentation: "Did not the advocates of our free school system," says Mr. Hopkins, Superintendent of Schools in Indiana, "promise the people, that, if they would take on their shoulders the additional burden of taxation for its support, the same would be lightened by the diminution of crime;

Is there any perceptible decrease of crime in Indiana? Is there any reasonable probability that there soon will be? It is becoming a grave question among those who take comprehensive views of the subject of education, whether this intellectual culture without moral is not rather an injury than a benefit. Is it not giving teeth to the lion, and fangs to the serpent? That is the true system of training which adapts itself to the entire complex nature of the child. No free government can safely ignore this grave subject, for nations that lose their virtue soon lose their freedom." Here is a remarkable statement by a friendly pen in the hand of the chief official of the educational department of Indiana, whose testimony, therefore, must be admitted as of great weight. Mr. Hopkins has been reading the newspapers of the day, and, startled by the revelations of crime among the intellectual and educated classes, who use the advantages of school learning the better to defraud creditors, embezzle trust funds, rob banks, form conspiracies to cheat the Government, and sell official honor for personal gain, is seeking some explanation of a condition of public and private morals that cannot continue without destroying the liberties of the Republic. He has hit on the right starting-point. Let him go on with his investigations, and fear not to disclose his discoveries.

WHAT IS SECULARISM?

Our argument is now with the secularists pure and simple. They point to their work accomplished, and bid us to the feast of rejoicing. We do not answer to the call, and stand ready to give the reason that is in us.

What is meant by secularism in schools? President Grant defines it to mean the exclusion from the schools of the teaching of any religious, atheistic or pagan tenet. Evidently the President has never been a school teacher, or has never tried to teach any thing save the multiplication table to a bright, intelligent boy, brought up in a Christian family on the plan here laid down. Commanding armies, handling a hundred thousand armed men, is child's play in comparison. God, Christ, sin, conscience, religion, heaven, hell, would meet him at every turn; and to flank them successfully, without insinuating a Christian, a pagan, or an atheistic tendency of thought, would give him more trouble than he experienced in outflanking the strongest army that ever met him on his onward marches.

"The Rochester Democrat and Chronicle," a stanch and zealous defender of secularism, gives its explanation as follows: "Strictly speaking, a secular school should not inculcate the belief in an overruling Providence."

The teacher who honestly means to teach according to the principles of secularism will find himself in continual embarrassment. If he but mention the name of God, of Christ, with reverence, he leads his bright pupils to infer that such a being exists; if he evades a question about God, he indicates doubt; if he speaks the name with a sneer on the lip, or a shrug of the shoulders, he inculcates to young, impressible minds his contempt for such a belief. Secularists must not attempt to escape the logic of their own demands. They ask, in the language of the President, the exclusion of all religious, atheistic, and pagan tenets from State schools; and where this doctrine lands them they must be pleased to stand. They scout the idea that merely excluding the Bible means secularism. This is the vain hope of evangelicals, and that with this concession they will be left free to make compilations from the Bible—elegant extracts—to keep up appearances. They do not comprehend the nature of the controversy. The dread of "popery" blinds them. They will not be let off without swallowing in all its bitterness this pill which they have helped prepare.

EVANGELICALS OBJECT TO THE TERM "GODLESS."

Yet some evangelical friends have been wrathy with me and others for designating the common schools, according to the new law, as Godless. I do not wish them to be Godless; it is not the fault of Catholics that they are becoming Godless. To leave our non-Catholic fellow-citizens free to settle the question of religious instruction in the schools to their own satisfaction, Catholics all over the country have provided, or they are providing, school accommodation for Catholic children, that the religious influences in these schools may be in harmony with the religious convictions of their patrons. Hardly had we made room in our own schools for all our Catholic children in the city of Rochester, than the board of education of the city, with little ceremony, put the Bible and all religious instruction out of the public schools. It was this board that made the schools under their care, in reality if not in name, Godless.

LIBERAL CHRISTIANS AND SECULARISTS.

The liberal Christian, led on by Henry Ward Beecher and a large body of clergymen of various evangelical denominations, fancies that morals can be taught, like good manners, on no higher ground or motive than the one of propriety or expediency. When interest, passion, the heart's cravings, outweigh propriety and expediency, morals thus taught go by the board.

The free religionist is at least consistent; consistency is more than the liberal evangelical Christian can claim. The former rejects the idea of a God-Creator, revelation, and all supernatural truths. He is justified in asking that his child shall not have its mind tinctured with such errors during school hours. He is resolute to drive out of the schools which he is taxed to support, and to which he sends his children, the sectarianism of evangelicalism; and he is equally determined to plant in them his pet doctrine, the sectarianism of secularism. It is the usual reading of history, that bodies of religionists never see themselves as others see them.

The religionist, Catholic and Christian, holding to divine and fixed truths, claims the right to impart a knowledge of these truths to his child in the school to which he sends it for education. The free religionist having no such truths to communicate to his child, insists that his fellow-citizens shall not be allowed to use the school-house for instruction in positive religion, because he sends his child to the same school. Thus, practically, he ostracizes the religion of the Christian, which is positive, and maintains his own, which is negative. All the gain is on the side of the free religionist, whose system of morals is so transcendental, and out of the reach of the masses, that it is valueless for practical good. Both call for the teaching of morals, and each in his own sense. The evangelical bases his notions of morality on the natural and revealed law; the free religionist, or secularist pure and simple, on the natural law, and as he conceives it. The latter would exclude the Sacred Scriptures and all positive religious teaching from the schools. Evangelicals are divided into two classes. One class would retain the Bible as a text-book of instruction in morals, as a sign of the Christianity of the schools, and as a mode of religious worship. They argue, with much truth, that if, owing to the neglect of parents at home, the insufficiency of the Sunday school and church to reach the children most in need of religious teaching, it be not imparted in the week-day school, it will never be imparted. Another class of evangelicals remit the Bible and all teaching of morals on religious grounds to the family, the Sunday school and the church; and join hands with the free religionists in prohibiting the name of God, of Christ, and of his teachings in the school. The least logical is this liberalized Christian evangelical who professes to teach morals without the authority in which he claims to believe. There is some justification for the stand taken by the former class of evangelicals and by free religionists; there is none for the position assumed by evangelicals who hold principles by which they care not to abide. The liberalized Christian and the free religionist assert that to be possible, which in the nature of things is not possible. The teacher does not exist who, in his schoolroom, can so divest himself of his own religious or irreligious ideas that no influence, direct or indirect, shall go out from him to his pupils. His very best efforts to escape the suspicion of sectarianism will only serve to tinge his teaching with indifferentism toward all religion; thus unintentionally, perhaps, responding to the wishes of the free religionist. Scudding from Scylla, he is wrecked on Charybdis, or *vice versa*.

On what ground, we may now ask, does either protest against the peculiar religious teachings of the other in State schools? Both are shocked that their taxes should be used to propagate religious creeds in which they do not believe. Neither has a word to say about the wrong perpetrated on the Catholic, whose taxes are used without stint to carry on a system of schools, from which he is kept out by their dominant evangelicalism or indifferentism.

A TRIANGULAR CONTEST.

Thus, as some declare, a triangular contest is inaugurated. "The Albany Argus" of Nov. 30, 1875, in reviewing a sermon of the Rev. Dr. Darling, in which the reverend doctor insists on keeping the Bible in the common schools, and because this is a Christian country, remarks, "Who shall decide? Shall the schools be secularized? Shall they be exclusively Christian, after the Darling model? Shall room be allowed for the McQuaid pattern of schools pervaded by Christian influences? The school question, then, does not bisect the community. It is a triangular contest, with the Darlings and McQuaids as allies and yet as antagonists; and with the secularists receiving strong support from Protestant pulpits, beside the partial support they receive from arguments such as are advanced by Dr. Darling." Three parties there are beyond doubt; but the contest can scarcely be called triangular. It is rather a struggle of three in one line, with the Catholic party in the middle. Each of the others has a hand in his pocket, taking his money to support schools to which he cannot in conscience send his children. If he but opens his mouth to complain, a din of angry sounds deafens him, and he gets more knocks than pence. His right to a conscience is admitted when his conscience conforms to the dictates of others. A few years ago his claim of conscientious convictions on the Bible question was derided. Now it is allowed. To-day he claims to educate his child in schools in harmony with his religious convictions. Neither contending party gives him heed. All point to the common schools, and while quarrelling among themselves as to what they are, and what they ought to be, bid him take them as they are, and as they have made them, or go his way, build his own schoolhouse, and please himself. This is moderate language; rougher and much less civil is what he hears. Strange to tell, however, no word is said of sending after him his money paid in school taxes. The ordinary principles of commercial honor are disregarded. The justice and equity required by the Constitution of Connecticut are ignored. Instead of justice the Catholic receives insults. "His money! It is the State's money, public money belonging to the State treasury, Protestant money. Be thankful that a generous people permits you to be blessed by the school advantages brought to your door."

WHO PAYS THE SCHOOL TAX?

Thus the poor Catholic, who may perchance have a little common-sense, hears, in the midst of loud talk about rights of man and rights of conscience, that his conscience is not his own, and the freedom offered him is somebody else's freedom; that his school taxes take on a special Protestant blessing as they drop into the common treasury, and may not come out without the odor of evangelicalism perfuming them. In downright derision he is asked, what taxes he pays? is he not a poor laborer, without a home he can call his own, a mere tenant-at-will? are not the taxes paid by the rich landlord? Simple and guileless the son of toil may be, and untutored in political economy, the laws of demand and supply, the intricacies of direct and indirect taxation; but his memory reminds him that when last the landlord called he was told that, as taxes and assessments had been so much increased, a trifle would have to be added to the rent. The same unpleasant remark met him in the grocery, the meat-shop, the shoe-store; wherever, indeed, he went to purchase the simplest necessaries of life. Anxious to learn how it was that the taxes had been augmented, he talked with his neighbors, and after many inquiries discovered that new and costly schoolhouses had been built, salaries of teachers and officials had been added to, and the sum of incidentals grown out of all proportion. A further study of the subject revealed the fact that one-fourth of all moneys raised by taxes in his town was needed for public schools. He then learnt why his rent was raised. He was not so dull that he could not comprehend, after the practical experience thus obtained, that the consumer and producer pay the taxes. The landlord the manufacturer, the seller draws the check in payment of the tax-bill; but the consumer and producer furnish a large part of the money with which to make good the check.

FALSE STATEMENTS AND ASSUMPTIONS.

This subject of State school education is overloaded with unfounded assumptions and incorrect statements. A prominent public man, clergyman, politician, or editor has scarcely given utterance to a plausible plea, when by the grand chorus of lesser oracles it is taken up and repeated, until it sounds like an accepted axiom.

WHAT IS SECTARIANISM?

The greatest abuse of language is in the popular meaning of the word "sectarian." On the frenzied brain of many it acts like the cry of "mad dog" in a crowded street. Who inquires into its signification? Light thrown on it would only weaken its power for mischief. The analyzation of the word by John C. Spencer, Secretary of State of New York, and one of the ablest lawyers the State has produced, dissects it thoroughly, and exposes the erroneous sense in which it is used. After saying that " Religious doctrines of vital interest will be inculcated, not as theological exercises, but incidentally in the course of literary and scientific instructions," and that such teachings are sectarian, he goes on to say, " It is believed to be an error to suppose that the absence of all religious instruction, if it were practicable, is a mode of avoiding sectarianism. On the contrary, it would be in itself sectarian, because it would be consonant to the views of a particular class, and opposed to the opinions of other classes. * * * His only purpose is to show the mistake of those who suppose they may avoid sectarianism by avoiding all religious instruction."

INCONSISTENCY OF THE EVANGELICAL.

Great confusion of ideas and grievous injustice result from this misapprehension of the sense of sectarianism. No one declaims so loudly against sectarianism as your intensely religious evangelical. Even when demanding that the Bible shall be read, and that his general form of Protestantism shall fill the schoolhouse, by some obliquity of mental vision peculiar to his class he startles the country by his frantic cries of danger to the public schools through sectarianism. Is this honest, or is it hypocritical? If the prejudices in which he was born and bred so confuse and blind his intellect that he cannot see a self-evident truth, his blunder may be charged to mistaken honesty. But what accumulated injustices spring out of his blunder!

BENIGNITY OF THE SECULARIST.

Then up rises the secularist, with benign countenance and gentle words, to reprove the evangelical for wrong done to the poor Catholic sectarian, and in the name of peace and conciliation, and as a settlement of all difficulties, to offer his gift of secularism pure and simple. It is not courteous to examine gifts too closely; but, as this one is bought partly with Catholic money, it must be borne with, that, before accepting the present, the Catholic turns it round on every side, scrutinizes its shape, its color, and its substance, to make sure that in it no danger lurks concealed. To the Catholic secularism is as much sectarian as evangelicalism.

AN AMERICAN'S RIGHT TO AGITATE.

A false statement, and one daily heard, is that to ask for a calm talk on the merits and demerits of the *existing system* of schools, means no less than an attempt to favor ignorance, impede education, and break down all schools. It is an American's right to argue, find fault, discuss, agitate. Agitation is healthful; in this particular instance, it quickens the building of Catholic schoolhouses. A Catholic is the last one to be taunted with want of love for education. He has only to point to his schools dotting the country from the Atlantic to the Pacific. All other classes put together do not equal him in number and efficiency of Christian Free Schools. Yet he is only at the beginning of his work.

NO DANGER FROM THE POPE.

Another incorrect statement is, that to allow parental rights, as demanded by the natural, the divine, and the common law, is to hand over the country to the pope and the Catholic Church, When the bigots of the country will permit the Government to deal with its citizens, the parents of the children, as equity and justice require, the liberties of the Republic will meet no danger from the Catholic Church or the pope. It is this bugbear of "popery" which bewilders and frightens people.

EXTENT OF COMMON-SCHOOL EDUCATION.

It is not decided what is meant by a common-school education. It is anything from A B C up to a finished university course, including professional studies except theology. Pres. Grant restricts it to the rudimentary branches of learning. Pres. Eliot of Harvard University, in "The Atlantic Monthly" of last June, makes this statement: "Suppose, for example, that the State requires of all children a certain knowledge of reading, writing, arithmetic and geography, such as children usually acquire by the time they are twelve years of age. It is not unreasonable, though by no means necessary, that the community should bear the whole cost of giving all children that amount of elementary training, on the ground that so much is necessary for the safety of the State; but, when the education of a child is carried above that compulsory limit, it is by the voluntary act of the child's parents, and the benefit accrues partly to the State, through the increase of trained intelligence among the population, but partly also to the individual, through the improvement of his powers and prospects."

Many of the secular newspapers agree with the above authorities, in limiting a common-school education to the simplest elementary branches. Such a restricted education answers for rural districts, in which a more extended course of studies is impossible. Tie down the curriculum of studies to the rudimentary branches of reading, writing, arithmetic and geography, in villages, towns, and cities, and in ten years' time the system of common schools will be abandoned. The ambition of all centres of population is to elevate the standard of common school education, until the town that cannot boast of its grammar school, and its high school, or day college, drops behind its sister towns in the race for advanced education at the public expense. The normal school, with its pretentious title, is another device for placing within the reach of large numbers, guiltless of any thought of following the teacher's profession, an education such as in former years could be had only in denominational academies and seminaries. To such an extent has this crowding-out of academies and seminaries, generally under denominational control, and supported by church organizations and private patrons, gone on, by the substitution of union schools, high schools, normal schools, free colleges, living on the bounty of the common treasury, that many denominational institutions have ceased to live, and others are only gasping for breath.

UNLIMITED EXPANSION OF THE SYSTEM.

Let us listen to two other authorities giving their opinion of the scope of common school studies. Henry Ward Beecher may be pitted against Pres. Grant, and Supt. Philbrick of Boston against Pres. Eliot. "The common schools," says Mr. Beecher, "should be so comfortable, so fat, so rich, so complete, that no select school could live under their drippings." In his annual report for 1874, Mr. Philbrick writes, "Our public schools are maintained on so liberal a scale, and their influence so largely predominates, that the private schools exert no appreciable effect upon their character." Boston has its system of Latin schools, normal schools, high schools, grammar schools, to demonstrate the absurdity of Pres. Grant's expectation that the rudimentary branches would satisfy the American people. Mr. Philbrick gives statistics to show, that, while in 1830 there were in Boston 7,430 children in the public schools, there were in private schools 4,018; but in 1873, with an addition of 200,000 to the population, there were in public schools 35,930, and in private schools only 3,887. Neither enumeration includes the 5,000 children in Christian free schools supported by parents of the Catholic religion.

WHY THEY DIFFER.

When the aim of the argument is to catch popular applause, we boast of a system of schools that brings to every child in the land a knowledge of the rudimentary branches of learning. When we wish to conciliate and win the patronage of well-to-do citizens in cities and towns, we impress on their minds the economy of obtaining superior education, including ancient and modern languages, and all the accomplishments, under the State arrangement, rather than in private schools. The public school system, as advocated by many to be imposed on all the citizens of this Republic, is nothing else, in my judgment, than a huge conspiracy against religion, individual liberty and enterprise, and parental rights. It is a monopoly on the part of the State, usurping to itself the entire control of the teacher's business, driving out competition, herding the children together in large numbers, working all alike as so many bits of machinery, instead of having them in smaller family and neighborhood schools, acting on the children according to individual character, by teachers more immediately under the control of parents.

Various causes work to push school taxation to an unbearable degree. Friends of common schools, taking advantage of popular sympathy, urge outlays of money for houses, apparatus, books, novelties of every kind, and increased salaries of teachers, so that tax-payers are at last asking to know what was the original contract, and where these enormous expenditures are to end; they are also looking for results, and comparing notes with other countries. Mr. Philbrick of Boston, when in Vienna, did not discover that our lavish disbursements of a good-natured people's money had given us a high rank in school progress, as compared with European countries, except in our primary schools.

COSTLINESS OF COMMON SCHOOLS.

But business men long ago learned that no job was so expensive as a government job; and no wonder that they are now turning their attention to this monopoly of State education, as a financial interest of general and deep concern in these hard times. There are others who can give figures and statistics of school work beside State and city superintendents of public schools. The Cincinnati correspondent of "The New York Daily Bulletin," a paper strictly commercial, writes under date of Jan. 17, 1876:

"Our schools, the best of our institutions, represent, for instance, fully as much miseducation as education; and the boards having charge of them are, compared with other bodies, least regardful of proper economy, because they act under a popular, and therefore the least analyzed, public feeling. If you will examine, you will find that, of all taxes, school taxes have for that reason increased fastest. Compare our school expenses with those of any German state, and you will find that ours cost more and perform least. The heaviest taxed German state for these purposes is Hesse Cassel; it taxes 34 cents per head, and it makes up 7½ per cent. of all the taxes levied. Now, there are levied for school purposes in Cincinnati $774,894, which is full $2.50 per head, and is about one-sixth of all the taxes, or 16 per cent. In Hesse Cassel the tax includes libraries, universities, and art schools: with us it includes only the schools up to high schools, and a good part of their expense is borne by trust funds. As to the culture, the German schools reach a larger proportion of the youth of the State, and are very thorough from the lowest to the highest grade, the teachers being much better qualified than ours. Had I taken Saxony or Baden, both more economical and efficient than Hesse Cassel, the comparison would have been still more against us. Zurich, the highest taxed city in Europe for these objects, takes but 54 cents per head, and there school taxes are one-fifth of all taxes; but there also it includes libraries, a university, polytechnicism, lyceums, and common schools; and surely no city on earth has a superior culture than this city."

Strongly as this writer puts his case, he fails to do it justice; for he omits to state that more than half the children of the city in schools are in parents' schools, or denominational and private schools. In New York City, school taxes are four dollars per head for each one of its million inhabitants; and large numbers of its children are in other than State schools. Boston, which has a less number of pupils in private and religious schools, shows a marked increase in the *per capita* cost. In 1873, for teachers and incidental expenses, not including new schoolhouses, the cost per head of its two hundred and fifty thousand inhabitants was $5.52; and, including the buildings, it reached nearly $7. These figures are for tax-payers.

Let me say to you just here, that if the scheme of higher education extending from the elementary school up to a full university course, now broached, be attempted to be carried out in its fullness and universality, all the revenues of all your cities, towns, and States, and all the revenues of these United States, will not suffice to pay the cost.

Intelligent, wise, earnest parents, and friends of sound education, will watch with interest the gradual unfolding and development of the State system of schools. Their attention will be given to this crushing-out of denominational schools for the humbler classes of society, to see in it the inexorable destruction of all denominational seminaries, academies, colleges, and universities.

STATE COLLEGES TO CRUSH OUT DENOMINATIONAL COLLEGES.

This policy is foreshadowed in the proposed National University scheme. I am not drawing inferences from my imagination. The address of Pres. White of Cornell University, delivered at Detroit, in August, 1874, lacks nothing in openness and directness of speech. Among other points, it contains these: "It is in view of such a meagre growth in over two hundred years, under the prevailing system, that I present the following as the fundamental proposition of this paper:

"*The main provision for advanced education in the United States must be made by the people at large, acting through their National and State Legislature, to endow and maintain institutions for the higher instruction, fully equipped and free from sectarian control.*

"*But I argue next, that our existing public school system leads us logically and necessarily to the endowment of advanced instruction.*"

To show his utter contempt for the rudimentary education called for by President Grant, Mr. White thus expresses his conviction: "The preliminary education which many of our strongest men received leaves them simply beasts of prey. It has simply sharpened their claws and tusks; but a higher education, whether in science, literature, or history, not only sharpens the faculties, but gives him new exemplars and ideals." President White and Herbert Spencer both require very advanced education before morals, under this new dispensation, avail to make a man better.

NO COLLEGES BUT STATE COLLEGES.

Mr. White's address is not a string of propositions and arguments without conclusions. Here is one:

"Next, as to State policy, I would have it go in the same direction as heretofore, but with a liberality and steadiness showing far more foresight. I would have each of those States build up higher, upon the foundations laid by national grants, their public institutions for advanced instruction as distinguished from private sectarian institutions.

"I would have each State build up one institution under its control, rather than the twenty under the control of conferences, and dioceses, and synods, and consistories, and presbyteries, and denominational associations of various sects."

There can be no mistake about the learned President's meaning, nor is one denominational organization omitted from his comprehensive catalogue. He advocates secularism, pure and simple, in our colleges and universities, paid for by taxes levied on the laborers, mechanics, and farmers of the country. He excludes from State aid all institutions in which any religious tenet, even the existence of an overruling Providence, is taught. If, on the establishment of these secular State colleges, their authorities should permit the reading of the Bible, as a book of spiritual or religious truths of more value than the Koran, it will be the cheerful duty of the Liberal League to protest against the abuse and infraction of the law, as the League protested in Philadelphia, "The use of the Bible in the public schools is a violation of the recognized American principle that the State and Church ought to be absolutely separate."

HOW WILL THE EVANGELICALS LIKE IT?

What will the members of the New England Baptist Educational Convention, assembled in Worcester, Mass., who recommended the establishment of at least one academy under Baptist control in each of the New England States, say to this arrangement? What will their brethren assembled in Chicago, and representing the Western States, think of it? How will the Southern Baptists who met in Marion, Ala., and who declared that "the only hope is Christian education in our schools," like a policy destined to overshadow and destroy denominational high schools, academies, and colleges as it destroyed denominational elementary schools? These three conventions were held in 1871. Pres. Andrews of Denison University, O., has the advantage of four years' experience and observation, since the holding of these conventions. He has seen the clouds gathering; he has heard the mutterings of the brewing storm ; the signs in the heavens tell him, that, when that storm bursts, it will be over the heads of denominational colleges. "The proposed reform," says Pres. Andrews, "will involve religious complications. Higher education cannot be separated from religion. Atheists will not pay taxes to support theistic instruction, nor theists atheistic. But to put higher instruction into the hands of the government is not only impolitic, but wrong in principle. * * * The government should hold the same relation to higher education that it does to religion. Further, religion is essential to higher culture, and the State cannot teach religion. It is injustice to those opposed to Christianity. Christianity is the natural ally of culture. Finally intellectual culture without religion cannot build character. The great need of the nation is moral force. The divorce of culture and religion is forced and unnatural." Does Pres. Andrews hope to avert the storm by his weak voice? Does he dream of holding the inner line of fortifications, protecting his higher education, after abandoning to the enemy all the outposts? When elementary schools, in which the foundation of sound Christian morals is laid, were given over to secularists at their first bidding, resistance to the advancing foe became impossible.

WHAT THE METHODISTS THINK.

In 1873, the Methodist Episcopal Church, in the quadrennial address of its bishops, thus put itself on record : "We do not hesitate to avow that we regard the education of the young as one of the leading functions of the Church, and that she cannot abdicate in favor of the State without infidelity to her trust and irreparable damage to society. The reasons for occupying this ground, which inhere in the very nature of this interest, and in the relation of children to the Church, all are intensified by the antagonism of modern science, and the outcasting of the religious element from all the school systems fostered by State legislation. It is not ours to dispute with Cæsar; but, fully persuaded that the salt of religious truth alone can preserve education, we feel that the responsibilities of the Church grow with the progress of society and the demands of the age."

WHAT MAKES THE METHODISTS CRAZY.

Other authorities of high standing in the Methodist denomination might be cited in favor of religious teaching in schools. It is but fair to state that the mention of any system of schools under which common justice might be meted out to Catholic parents, suffices to drive the whole body of Methodist preachers and hearers frantic, crazy. The Baptists are not much less intolerant. Secularists may therefore count on their assistance in ousting from the schools the very name of the Christians' God. The professed principles of these religious sects avail nothing against their avowed hatred of the Catholic Church and Catholics.

WHO SUPPORT CHURCHES?

The various evangelical sects yielded up the contest for religious education in common schools almost without a struggle. It is said that the children, whose education is not advanced beyond the elementary branches of learning, do not in time become pew-holders and supporters of churches. These efficient aids to church support are found in the classes which pass through denominational schools of a higher grade. Round these all the forces of evangelicalism will rally to uphold the right of parents of the respectable class to provide religious education for their children. Certainly the zeal, the labors, the munificent generosity, of the evangelical denominations, to build and endow academies and colleges deserves unbounded praise. But when the State opens its plethoric treasury to establish secular colleges, with allowances of freedom not possible in sectarian institutions, the struggle will be short and decisive. This is not prophecy; it is history.

WHAT KILLS EVANGELICAL COLLEGES?

The once flourishing Methodist College at Lima, N.Y., dwindled to insignificance, and moved to Syracuse to escape death, shortly after the opening of Cornell University. About the same time, Hobart College, under the control of the Episcopal Church, began to lose students, until now, notwithstanding large endowments, the fingers of the two hands would almost suffice to count them. The Presbyterian Seminary of Geneseo closed its doors when a State normal school in the same village opened its classes. The Baptist Academy of Brockport became a State normal school to escape death. Other places have the same history. The atmosphere of these normal schools is still redolent with evangelicalism, but it is only on sufferance; at the first demand of Jew or atheist the names of the God, Creator, and Christ will be banished, praying and hymn-singing stopped.

I now leave Evangelical Christians to ponder over Pres. Grant's demand that no religious tenet shall be taught in State schools, and this new definition of non-sectarianism.

SECULARISTS ARE IN GREAT GLEE

over their progress. They look forward to speedy and complete success. Their victory in common schools carries them triumphantly along to State secular universities. Indeed, they might begin their song of triumph, if not for complete accomplishment, then for rapid advancement. Only one foe stands undismayed before them. It is the Catholic parent who permits no one to come between him and his child. The father is a Christian, prizing his faith more than his purse or the world's esteem; resolute to transmit to his offspring the precious boon of religion in its purity and brightness, undimmed by the jeers and scoffs and calumnies of unbelievers; he will not permit his children to breath an atmosphere of infidelity. Others may think and say that he is wrong: he knows that he is right. He meddles not with others. He listens to much counsel from well-meaning friends. They tell him it is a glorious privilege for his boy to be the equal and companion of a rich man's son. It may happen —it often happens—that he cares no more for the rich man's son than for the rich man himself. They point to the palatial school-house, grand and gorgeous in all its appointments; to the teachers, learned and accomplished. They tell him all these shall his son enjoy, without price or pay, if he will but intrust his boy's education to the State, which loves to play foster-father to its children. The poor man's poverty gnaws into the bone under the proffered bribe; his mind dwells on the temporal advantages so enticingly offered; he loves his child, and he believes in an overruling Providence, a God, Creator, Supreme Master of the universe; he believes in a world to come, and cherishes the hope that, after this life, he and his boy shall be reunited with the blessed in heaven. Under the coarse coat and rough exterior of many a day-laborer there beats a heart of honest manliness that would scorn to be the beneficiary of any man's aid. He pays for his child's education; he hates to pay for a superior education for his richer neighbor's son. There is a laudable pride in this spirit of independence and self-reliance, the very virtues upon which the Republic depends for its existence.

He can conceive of no true happiness except as his life conforms to the teachings and will of his God. His thoughts of happiness for himself are bound up with those of his child. His child's happiness for this world and the next interests and determines his actions at home, in its play, in school, and in church. He is concerned about its lessons, but still more about every influence bearing on the direction and formation of mind and character. Like Herbert Spencer, he knows that mere intellectual education will not form character; and, like Pres. White, he holds that the preliminary education which many receive "only sharpens claws and tusks, and makes beasts of prey." To guard against such dangers, this father, whose religion is real and living, made up of doctrines to be known and believed, and of observances and practices to be faithfully followed, dares not before God and his conscience neglect to train his son in these observances, make him familiar with their use, and fill his mind and soul with love and reverence toward them. How will it be with his boy, if the school fail to come to his aid, or, what is worse, operate disastrously, by positive or negative teaching, upon his soul? What will be the future of that boy if the atmosphere he breathes at school be filled with doubt, sneers, negation? There is not in this audience one father, who, if he believed in a life to come, of happiness or misery eternal, would take any unnecessary chances with regard to his child's education and school life. If you judge the rest of the world only from your standpoint of belief, the brave struggle of a Catholic poor man to obtain a Christian education for his child will continue to be an enigma, and lead to acts of injustice.

AGREEMENTS AND DISAGREEMENTS.

Catholics and secularists agree on some points, and differ on others.

They agree that education is an important factor in the making of an intelligent citizen, and is therefore very desirable. They do not agree in the character of the education necessary to make this good citizen. The Catholic points to his personal sacrifices in time, labor, and money, to secure for his children education in the sense in which he understands it. The secularist bids us look at what the State has done for him. He cannot demonstrate the earnestness and sincerity of his convictions and preaching by what he has done. He pays, it is true his share of public taxes. So does the Catholic. The secularist insists that there shall be State schools after his plan, according to his convictions, paid for by taxation from which no one shall be exempt, while all shall be obliged to drink at his well of knowledge, such as it is. A Catholic argues that the secularist's notion of education was never strong, never attained to the power of a principle, or he would have withdrawn his children from schools in which they were taught what he might be pleased to call the superstitions of evangelicalism. As between the two, on the head of personal sacrifices in furtherance of the cause of education, the Catholic has an advantage over the secularist in demonstrating the courage of his convictions.

Both agree that instruction in morals in some form is essential for the right education of youth. They differ in their understanding of what is meant by morals, and as to the authority by which such teaching should be inculcated. The secularist rises no higher in his conception of morals than the temporal well-being of the child, and "the doing of acts conducive to general enjoyment." Rev. A. D. Mayo, Unitarian minister, calls this policy "a materialistic naturalism and a philosophical fatalism."

SECULARISTS TEACHING MORALS.

The helplessness of the secularist as a teacher of the people is best described by Herbert Spencer in "First Principles:" "Few, if any, are as yet fitted wholly to dispense with such (religious) conceptions as are current. The highest abstractions take so great a mental power to realize with any vividness, and are so imperative on conduct unless they are vividly realized, that their regulative effects must, for a long period to come, be appreciable on but a small minority.... Those who relinquish the faith in which they have been brought up, for this most abstract faith in which religion and science unite, may not uncommonly act up to their convictions. Left to their organic morality, enforced only by general reasonings imperfectly wrought out and difficult to keep before the mind, the defects of nature will often come out more strongly than they would have done under their previous creed." No one is better entitled to a hearing on the side of the secularists than Herbert Spencer. How far they are able to provide a code of morals for the training of the young in substitution of that of the Christian religion, he has clearly stated. The child accepts its lessons in science and morals on authority. The secularist child has no other authority than that of the teacher, supplemented and enforced by its parents. Hence the necessity of harmony of thought between parent and teacher. But "moral goodness," to be effective even in the secularist's idea, demands vividness of conception beyond the power of attainment on the part of children, since few of their parents can rise to its realization. In other words, the teaching of morals in a secularist's school is all but impossible.

STANDARDS OF MORALS DIFFER.

The secularist's standard of morals differs in material points from that of the Catholic. The former, in admitting the law of divorce, consents to a disruption of ties that alone guarantee the sacredness and unity of the family; permits passion, pleasure, and self-will to have their way in defiance of that law of self-restraint and patience under trials and difficulties necessary to hold the family together, at least for the children's sake. The Catholic can address the secularist in the words of the eloquent Bishop of Orleans: "It is not so much *my church* which they would destroy as *your home;* and I defend it. For all those things which are the supreme objects of your desire,—reason, philosophy, society, the basis of your institutions, the subject of your books, the sanctity of your hearts, the morals of your children,—these are the things which I defend, and which you throw away in crowning those who would destroy them."

A Catholic's code of morals embraces the teachings of the Bible, interpreted by the Church. It does not end with teachings; it has ordinances, sacraments divinely instituted to give grace, supernatural power, with which to resist temptation, overcome passion, escape from sin. Your denial of these truths does not lessen a Catholic's faith in them, nor weaken his conscience with regard to them.

You may remember Henry Ward Beecher's last Thanksgiving sermon, and the picture he drew of the condition of morals in the Brooklyn schools, in which were teachers who held their positions by the sacrifice of their virtue to school commissioners. You may also have heard that Thomas W. Field, superintendent of schools in the same city of Brooklyn, in his annual report of four or five years ago, gave a fearful account of the prevalent immorality. This report was suppressed by the board of education, on the principle, I suppose, that the whole truth must not always be spoken. Is it any wonder that Catholic parents ask that they, and not politicians, shall have the choosing of their children's teachers? You have not forgotten the article in "The Boston Herald" of Oct. 20, 1871, giving the substance of Prof. Agassiz' address before the Massachusetts State Teachers' Association. Again, I say, is it any wonder that Catholic parents, hearing these confessions, even under a stringent policy of silence and concealment, lose faith in the State system, and provide schools of their own at sacrifices worthy of martyrs? I cite these instances in no spirit of exultation, but of regret; and it therefore gives me pleasure to say that the character of the teachers of Boston stands too high to come under such imputations.

THE STATE CANNOT TEACH RELIGION.

Catholics and secularists agree that a State without religion cannot teach religion. Therefore, say the latter, let there be no religious teaching. Therefore, say the former, let there be religious teaching in the schools by those who can impart it in harmony with the parents' belief. These say furthermore, that, when Massachusetts had religion, she was careful that religion, and morality through religion, should be taught in our schools. It is claimed that Massachusetts gained her most distinguished honors from men educated under religious influences in school, at home, and in church; but that now she is consuming her capital, without putting any of it at interest. The shadow of religious teachings still lingers around her schoolhouses. Shall it be that her future men of note are to be no more than shadows of those that went before them?

MORALS WITHOUT RELIGION.

The secularist maintains that all the knowledge of morals a child need possess may be obtained in a State school without religion. This is true of that species of morals which fails to recognize God, and which has no foundation in supernatural motives. The Catholic does not admit that morality based on pure selfishness is of much worth, or that it will avail a child in the moment of temptation. In this clashing of opinions and beliefs, which shall give way, is there to be room but for one? Shall it be the Catholic? He appeals to the Constitution of Massachusetts, and to the religious element still abiding in its population. The new condition of educational aims is vastly different from that of fifty years ago. He claims that his higher standard of morality, the nobler motive on which it is inculcated, its adaptability and acceptableness to children (waiving for a moment its divine origin and character) entitles him to have the education of his children permeated and completed by a strong infusion of religious instruction in schools. He contends for the rights and best interests of his own children. He does not dispute the wishes of others, nor seek to impose on them the adoption of his system. He loudly asserts, that in every important point, except costliness of buildings and expensiveness of teachers, Catholic schools are superior to State schools. They are more thorough in secular studies, there is less cramming, and less multiplicity of useless branches of learning; the duties and responsibilities of citizens are brought home to parents, where they belong, fostering a spirit of self-reliance, without dependence on public charity; and all in an atmosphere of religion and morality such as the patrons of the school desire, and are willing to pay for. I am not speaking of the beginnings of a Catholic school in some poor neighborhood. As well might you liken a country school with its fifteen or twenty scholars under a schoolmistress at three or four dollars a week, to one of your Boston high schools.

CATHOLICS ASK NO FAVORS.

While the Catholic asks no favor, no privilege, no special prerogative, no right that he does not concede to others, the secularist on the contrary, in the name of liberality, falls into astonishing illiberality. All must yield to him. He has broken down the evangelical; he will subdue the Catholic. He will concede no rights to others, save the one of bending to his will, if that can be called a right which is the result of sheer force, through the power of a prejudiced and unrelenting majority. The Catholic wants to know why his right to have schools for his children, in which the tone of religious thought shall be Catholic, is not as valid as the right of evangelicals and secularists to have schools for their children in which the tone of thought shall be evangelical or indifferent to any religion. It must not be lost sight of, in this argument, that our rights go where our money goes. A Catholic's money goes into the schools, and his rights go with it. An inalienable right is infringed upon, is curtailed, is cut off altogether, when he appears at a schoolhouse door, leading his son by the hand, only to find at its threshold the emblem or sign of a hostile creed, or, what is worse in his belief, the chilling atmosphere within of doubt, negation, or an ignoring of the God-Creator, Sovereign Lord and Master, and final Judge of man's thoughts, words, and acts, for whom it has been the father's duty to instil into his child's mind and heart the most tender love and reverence.

HOW SOME ARE SAVED.

No one need tell me that I exaggerate and picture from fancy, nor yet again that there are illustrious instances of boys and girls that have passed through the common schools without inhaling the poisonous atmosphere of which I speak. I do not deny the fact. These easily counted exceptions but prove the rule. The prayers, the watchful care, and unceasing devotion of capable and pious parents, must count for much in the saving of these few. Again, there are schools, in which the majority of the children and many of the teachers being Catholics, a diluted Catholic atmosphere floats about the school-house, rendering less, in some degree, the danger of losing Catholic faith and morals. If we ourselves cannot see this danger, ministers and editors, in sermons, addresses, and editorials, kindly point it out, and bespeak our attention. Their zeal and ardor are aroused to new endeavor in the charitable hope of hurting "Popery." The thought lends courage to their hearers. "It will de-Romanize the children," says one. "The Bible and the common schools will grind out the Catholicity of the children," says another. Similar expressions might be multiplied without end. Forewarned is for the wise to be fore-armed. It was only when the Bible in the schools had ceased to be the question in dispute that the Bible was put on the cold side of the door.

WHAT RAISES THE STORM.

There is small hope that justice, or even patient and unbiased hearing of our grievances, will be accorded, when, as soon as a voice is raised in behalf of God-given rights, forty thousand pulpits ring with bitter invectives, gross misrepresentations, and appeals to the lowest passions of those who gather around them; when politicians, (not statesmen) catch up the cry, and trading away all principle, if they ever had any, ride into office in the fury and madness of the hour. Secret societies, that have so often proved political sepulchres for unprincipled demagogues, lend their help.

The darkest and fiercest hour of the storm is that which precedes its breaking. We take courage, then, from the extreme and unbridled fury of the hour, and from the violent language used in defiance of good taste, reason, brotherly kindness, and all regard for just rights.

LEADERS CHANGE.

The people will yet become disgusted with the unreasonableness and changeableness of their leaders. A few years ago they were told to stand by "the Bible in the schools," to "strike down any one who dared raise a hand against it;" that "to die for it would be a glorious martyrdom." Secret societies were formed for its protection. Now, editors and ministers frankly confess it was all a mistake; that our liberties do not depend on keeping the Bible in the schools; that to do so is illogical, wrong, unjust to Catholics, Jews and infidels. There has been no more powerful advocate of the Bible in the schools than Dr. J. G. Holland, who, in this month's "Scribner," admits that "the compulsory reading of the Bible was to the Catholic, to the Jew, to the atheist, a grievance, a hardship, an oppression." "For ourselves,' he says, "we must confess to a change of convictions on this matter.... If we do away with the grievance of the Catholic, we do away with his claim; and we mark out for Catholic and Protestant alike the path of peace to walk in side by side." The doctor does not seem to understand the nature of our claim. It is not to deprive Protestants of their Bible in their schools: it is to educate Catholic children in Catholic schools with our own money, under State supervison if you please. We do not want Protestant money, nor any State money that was not taken from our purses. We want not one dollar for pope, bishop, or priest · not one cent for our church. We do not desire the doing-away of common schools: we are establishing schools all over the country on a thoroughly democratic basis. We are striving for a stretching of a hide-bound system. We wish it to be more directly under parental control, more economically managed, restricted to its proper function of elementary education, and violating no conscientious duty of parents. It is just as likely that a few years hence the people will be told that education belongs to parents, and that if the State interferes it must be in accordance with the wish of parents. When communism becomes rife and bold, property owners may be willing to discuss principles only to learn that they are reaping as they sowed. Some heads take in truth slowly, others only by trepanning.

FAIR PLAY EXPECTED FROM FREE RELIGIONISTS.

We are justified in expecting fairer treatment at the hands of free religionists. If we may trust Herbert Spencer as a worthy exponent of this class, toleration in its widest sense is a fundamental dogma of their creed: "Our toleration should be the widest possible; or, rather, we should aim at something beyond toleration, as commonly understood. In dealing with alien beliefs our endeavor must be, not simply to refrain from injustice of word or deed, but also to do justice by an open recognition of positive worth. We must qualify our disagreement with as much as may be of sympathy" (First Principles).

From scientists and free religionists, then, we may expect the same rights they claim for themselves. As they would not consent to our forcing their children into schools under Catholic influences, direct or indirect, so they will not ask that our children shall be forced into schools under objectionable influences. As they do not permit us to decide upon the truth or untruth of their religious opinions, so they will not seek to decide for us upon our doctrines. Here comes in the apparently insurmountable obstacle to an amicable settlement of this vexed question. Each one of the disputants, except the Catholic, wants to make all others bend to his plan, or way, or system, seemingly satisfied that he alone is right. The Catholic, on the contrary, says, Let each one have his own plan; and with an even start, and on equal ground, let it be seen which party, the evangelical, the scientist, or free religionist, or the Catholic, can make the greatest sacrifices, accomplish the most work in the most satisfactory manner, for the thorough religious and secular education of all the children they can bring under their control.

NO RELIGION IN A BANK.

Free religionists, and the large class of Christian religionists represented by Henry Ward Beecher, answer, Religion has no place in the State school; and, with it kept out, the school is as free to one class of religionists as to another, and equally so to Jews and infidels. To illustrate this theory, they say that as there need be no religion in a bank, a shop, or a business office, so there need be no religion in a school. This is as strong a justification as they can bring.

The comparison fails for want of resemblance between the things compared. A man goes into the bank, the shop, the office. A boy goes to the school. The bank, the shop, the office, has for its object the transaction of its own special material business. The school deals with the boy's mind and heart; is a place set apart for the forming, disciplining, educating of the young, by trained and skilled manipulators of the intellect and emotions. The young look up to these teachers with sentiments of respect and often of reverence; nor are they capable of analyzing and judging the influences brought to bear on them. They are in the school six hours a day, for five days in the week, ten months in the year. They are justified in voting all schooling, in excess of these long hours, a bore. They who go into a bank, or any other place of business, are men grown, fully competent to judge of insidious or open attempts to prejudice their minds on points of religion or morals. These business offices are not monopolies like the State school, and their proprietors know the danger of meddling with their customers' religious opinions. The example of a man asking for a Bible in a hat-shop has not yet occurred; and, when it does occur, it will be met by calling in a policeman to arrest an escaped lunatic. But a child asking a teacher to tell it something about God, Christ, the redemption, sin, or a life to come, would ask a proper question, entitled to an answer from a competent teacher. Much as our opponents may be pleased to protest against religion in State schools, it is there, and in some shape it will be there till the end of time. I am not speaking of evangelical schools, but of schools purely secular, in which there is no Bible, no text book of religion, no prayer, no hymn; and yet, in this expurgated and shrivelled-up school, the teaching will be for or against religion, as the teacher happens to be. His children do not come to him to buy bills of exchange, or boots, or hats, but to acquire knowledge, to learn, to take in, through open eyes and ears, information concerning the things it sees, and the truths and facts of which it hears. Pres. Anderson, of Rochester University, is an authority in educational methods and means, of great weight wherever known. He exhibits this power of the teacher in a few striking passages, thus:—

PRESIDENT ANDERSON ON INCIDENTAL INSTRUCTION.

"With the element of Christian faith in head and heart, it is impossible for an earnest teacher to avoid giving out constantly religious and moral impulses and thoughts.

He must of necessity set forth his notions about God, the soul, conscience, sin, the future life, and divine revelation. If he promises not to do so he will fail to keep his word, or his teachings in science or literature or history will be miserably shallow and inadequate....Incidental instruction in morality and religion, then, ought to be the main reliance of the Christian teacher. The ends of a Christian school, while working by its own laws and limitations, ought not to be essentially different from a Christian church. The principles we have thus indicated are universal in their application. If the Christian teacher must make the elements of his religious faith color all his teaching, the same must be true of the unchristian teacher.... There is no good thinking that is not honest thinking ... If parents wish their children educated in Christian principles, they must seek out honest Christian men to be their teachers."

Here in a few words is the plainly spoken judgment of an experienced teacher. It is true, Pres. Anderson is contending in behalf of higher education in colleges and seminaries. But I do not hesitate to say, with no small experience as an educator, that in elementary schools, where young minds are dealt with, the incidental teaching in morals and religion is of vastly greater extent and effect. They who assert so boldly that children of inquisitive and unfolding minds can frequent schools for secular learning, without being influenced by the dominant religious tone of the school and the teachers, speak without warrant.

THE MULTIPLICATION TABLE.

As meaningless an illustration is that in which the multiplication table plays a part. There is no religion, they say, in the multiplication table. I never heard any one say there was, while it is not unknown that there may be religion, or antipathy to religion, in him who teaches the table, as well as in the place in which it is taught. A Sneer at "popery" requires no allusion to figures or ciphering, unless when the years of the Apocalypse, or the coming of Antichrist are under discussion.

A COMMON LANGUAGE.

But, after all, the vexed question of religion aside, see the gain to the Republic by giving a common language to all its children, through the common schools. Then why, if that is a gain, provide a teacher of German wherever a few German children are found, or, where there are many, give them a school with German as its language, as in Erie, Penn.? There is room for any thing and every thing except religion.

DOES THIS SYSTEM ABOLISH CASTE?

Anyhow, it cannot be denied, we are told, that the common schools bring all classes of children to the same level, make them men on equal ground, and sit side by side on the same benches. This speech belongs to the demagogue and the electioneering stump. The level spoken of may be found in rural districts and small towns; it is quite unknown in large cities in practice, while no one denies the beauty of the theory.

It is well known that in cities the rich, as a rule, live in neighborhoods where no poor man can have his home. When there is danger of contact, the rich man sends his daintily nurtured and well-clad child to a private school. There are public schools in New York and Brooklyn, whose pupils come solely from the comfortable classes. What an advantage to the pride of so many admirers of common schools, that thirty thousand children of laborers and mechanics in New York, and twenty thousand in Brooklyn, are educated in Christian free schools! It makes access to the public schools so much the more pleasant. Why is it that so many thousand children receive their elementary education not in the public schools, but in the schools of the Children's Aid Society, under evangelical influences? Is it not beyond doubt that if in New York City the compulsory law were to be enforced, and all the children now running the streets, and all the children now in the Aid Society's schools, and all the children now in the Catholic free schools, were to be marched into their district public schools, an almost equal number of well-dressed children would be marched out? If in any school the influence of money and good society predominates, the poor will quit it for shame's sake; if patched pants and calico dresses rule, the rich will go out for pride's sake. You will find truer democracy in the Christian free schools of New York than in the common schools.

SCHOOL HOURS AND SCHOOLMASTERS.

The week-day school, we are told, is not the place for teaching religion; there are hours enough for these lessons at home and on Sunday. This advice comes with a bad grace from Boston, since the Medical College of Middlesex has laid down these two rules among others: "The duration of daily attendance, including the time given to recess and physical exercises, should not exceed four and a half hours for the primary schools." "There should be required no study out of school for children of the primary schools."

A more serious consideration is that of compelling parents to be schoolmasters to their children. It is cruel to put this task on backs already overburdened. Father and mother toil like slaves from morning to night. Do their mentors think of the early rising, the hasty breakfast, the long hours of wearying and exhausting labor, of the fatigued frame that at the coming on of night seeks needed rest? We are not speaking in favor of clerks, merchants, and professional men. They can speak for themselves and their requirements; their friends are numerous, intelligent, and active. Legislation always takes their circumstances and wants into account.

It is among the laboring and mechanic classes that a numerous progeny is found. The mother sees to her household and the wants of her many children. Her education in book-learning may be defective; and, if she undertook to compete with the trained schoolmistress, her deficiencies might become known to her young ones. Time, strength, capacity—all are wanting. Yet she is reminded, if she reads the newspapers, that one minister and another devote their time to set and formal religious instruction of their children, out of school, in the evenings, on the Saturdays, and with special care on the Sundays; and she is piously advised to do the same. These learned, eloquent, leisured clergymen put themselves on a par with the hard-working mason and the humble washerwoman. It is, I say, an unworthy mockery of these respectable bread-winners, day-workers, or betrays profound ignorance of their conditions and daily occupations. These poor people pay their taxes to have others in whom they have confidence, whose religious convictions harmonize with their own, relieve them of a duty they feel incompetent to perform. The Sunday-school and the Church remain. Good children go to Sunday school; those whose home are least Christian in spirit and teachings keep clear of it. Besides, who would be satisfied to have his child put off with one lesson a week in any of the rudimentary branches belonging to the common school? Yet the lesson of lessons, the law and will of God as manifested to his creatures, by which character is formed and moral principles are well established, may be satisfactorily learned in the short hour of a Sunday-school.

Parents need the Church and the best services of the clergyman on Sunday more than their children, that they may not forget the lessons of their youth.

THE SPECIAL ADVANTAGES OF CATHOLIC SCHOOLS.

It seems more than unreasonable to ask Catholic parents to forego advantages attainable in and through Catholic schools,—advantages far superior to any offered by State schools.

First, Catholic schools instruct in all the useful branches of a sound English education.

Secondly, They are more economical, costing no more than one-fourth or one-third the expense of supporting State schools; and commanding at the lowest possible price, merely food and clothing, one of the most expensive necessities of the age and country,—skilled and trained intellectual labor.

Thirdly, Their teachers are devoted to their work of teaching as a life-work; study every day, and waste no time in idle visits and foolish amusements.

Fourthly, These teachers are in sympathy with the religious faith of the patrons of their schools.

Fifthly, Parental schools alone will stand the test of logic; they are consonant to sound democratic republican doctrines;

they make possible the inculcation of morality by the authority of a divine Lawgiver; they respect the natural rights of parents, and meddle with and infringe on no one else's rights.

They are a necessity demanded by the circumstances of the times, and the demoralized condition of the country, as well as for the future welfare of the Republic. It is our common country, belonging not to one man more than to another. He is the best citizen, no matter where he was born, who loves it most and labors in his sphere of life, according to his ability, with purest motives, for the honor and prosperity of the Union. He would be a renegade and base betrayer of his country, who, believing that morality on a religious foundation was essential to the safety and continuance of the government, should consent to withhold from children all possible means of growth in sound moral principles and conduct.

RIGHTS OF MINORITIES IN OTHER COUNTRIES.

The experience of every civilized nation of Europe is against the suicidal career that we are entering on. No difficulty is found in countries whose inhabitants are of different religious beliefs, in arranging a system of schools for all. Though some of these countries are spoken of as despotic in character, their despotism never goes so far as to interfere with the religious convictions of Catholic, Jew, or evangelical. At least Catholic Canada, our immediate neighbor, Catholic Belgium, Catholic France, Catholic Bavaria, and Catholic Austria, respect the parental rights of the minority, with a sense of justice we would do well to study. The wisdom and good sense of the world are not concentrated in the American people.

THE QUESTION MUST BE SETTLED.

This question, thanks to various causes, is now fairly before the country for discussion and settlement. To shelve it by constitutional amendments will be no lasting settlement. Constitutional enactments in contravention of parental rights not transferred to the State are worth the parchment on which they are written, and no more. This is not an original idea. I have picked it up in Boston. This lesson was taught to the nation by the settlement of slavery.

POLITICAL PARTIES.

The agitation, I must confess, is embarrassing to both political parties; much more so, however, to political aspirants who fear pitfalls, and are anxious lest they bury all their hopes in graves of their own digging. One party is rushing along on its path of injustice, because popular clamor impels that way; the other, half willing, half unwilling, does not dare say a word in opposition, for it, no more than the other party, has statesmen for leaders, while politicians abound. We are accused of an alliance with one of these parties. The party that forms an alliance, open or covert, with any religious body in these United States, proclaims its own folly, and signs its own death-warrant. The leaders of the Catholic body are neither fools to trust any political party, nor knaves to seek privileges and favors over the religious denominations of the country by such unworthy and dishonorable means. No prominent politician believes the absurd imputation. It is a sop thrown to Cerberus, to bigotry. We seek equal rights for all, favors for none. Until correct principles obtain recognition, this question, affecting the interests of millions of citizens, will remain a cause of controversy and disturbance. Thirty years of patient submission have brought us scarcely a kindly word; and the condition of helotism into which we have been falling is regarded by many as fitting and proper, and by others as right and just. There is a sound maxim in the American mind, that any class suffering from disabilities and a violation of rights should resort to established methods for a rectification of these wrongs, and that a class that does not care enough to seek a remedy for its sufferings may be left to nurse its grumblings in private, without thought or attention from their fellow-countrymen.

While, therefore, we do not feel disposed to waste gratitude on the Democratic party for favors never received, and owe no more to the Republican party, we have only contempt for the hangers-on of both parties, who would have us hold in abeyance the assertion of our rights, lest this office-seeker or another should be embarrassed. Catholics are learning to break away from both parties, watch events, and treasure in their memories the brave words and deeds of politicians who, taking advantage of a momentary outbreak of bigotry and religious hate, write a record which a few years hence they would give their right hand to blot out.

CHARGES AGAINST THE SYSTEM.

We charge upon the system of State schools, as now carried in these United States, the perpetration of manifold injustices and the upholding of false principles.

First, It is an infringement of parental rights and duties, inasmuch as it compels poor people who educate their own children for conscience' sake, to help educate their richer neighbors' children.

Secondly, It cruelly oppresses poorer citizens by giving to their richer neighbors' sons not simply an elementary education, but an education sufficient to earn their living by means of a learned profession. To put both on an equal footing, poor children should be taught a trade at the expense of the State.

Thirdly, The State does not know what its system should be. In some States, the education is restricted to rudimentary studies; in others, it extends to a university course. Some States allow a qualified amount of evangelical teaching; others, professing to exclude all religion, permit any except the Catholic. These are the inconsistencies and hypocrisy of the system.

Fourthly, It is narrow, contracted, limited in its scope, afraid of rivalry, and incapable of the very function for which it was established. Its right to educate is denied by its admission that it cannot educate in the true sense of the word.

Fifthly, It stultifies itself; for, beginning on a religious basis, and acquiring its chief renown by the fruits of its first work, it would end by banning and barring all religious beliefs, even "the existence of an overruling Providence."

Sixthly, It establishes a monopoly of a business best left to individual enterprise and the immediate control of parents.

Seventhly, The principles on which it is justified will justify with greater force the claim of the communist to labor and bread.

ADMIT THE WRONG, AND CHANGE THE SYSTEM.

After so much fault finding with the *existing system* of common schools, it is not out of the way to ask what system is proposed in exchange. My object is not to propose plans and systems, but to argue that the present one is radically wrong, and needs amendment. Until the American people admit the failure of the system as it now is, no change need be looked for. Once admitted, they will be quick to bring about a change. They will either throw education directly and compulsorily on parents, paying only for those unable to pay for themselves, or they will so broaden the system that all can come under it without the sacrifice of conscientious rights. This plunging into secularism is only the cowardice of the politician who fears to face the consequences of sound logic, common-sense, equal rights, parental prerogatives, and a secretly nourished hatred and conspiracy against the Catholic Church. To put off justice in deference to the expediency of the hour, is the way of the politician: the statesman announces his principles, and stands or falls by them. Truth is old; it is ever new; it endures forever.

FULL DISCUSSION AND FAIR ARGUMENT.

I appear before you at your request. On one point at least we agree. It is your good pleasure to listen to arguments in favor of principles and doctrines with which you do not agree because in your judgment they are not sound. You do not, on that account, question my honesty of purpose, my sincerity of conviction, or my love of country. Perhaps the speaker of this afternoon and his hearers are as wide apart on this question as any two individuals in the country. Yet we have come together, —I, to address you in plainness of speech, not wanting, I trust, in courtesy; you, to listen patiently and attentively.

BOSTON SHOULD SETTLE THE QUESTION.

When designing men are plotting mischief and breeding hate and rancor, it is well for Boston to furnish this useful lesson to other parts of the country.

To you, men of Boston, to the intelligence and honesty of Massachusetts, and especially of Boston, I, in my character of Catholic American citizen, appeal in behalf of the rights of parents for dispassionate consideration of this subject; confident that, if not heeded to-day, the day is not distant when it will be considered. I have said it before, I say it again, that the settlement of this great question, affecting the future welfare and stability of the Republic, must come from Boston and Massachusetts. It is more creditable, in the mean time, for us to suffer, to be punished and persecuted, than for American citizens to persecute. The rights you would maintain at any cost for yourselves, I beseech you not to deny to the humblest citizens in the land, however helpless they may seem. For large numbers, who have few to speak for them, I plead before you. Your interests and theirs, as fellow-citizens, are bound together as one. Our country is with unparalleled quickness becoming one of populous cities. These centres of population, notwithstanding extraordinary efforts to counteract the danger, are nurturing street Arabs, wild youths, bands of trained depredators on others' property, hosts of corrupt, demoralizing inhabitants. Peaceable and order-loving citizens are bound for their own sake to look at the danger, call to their assistance every available agency, and engage the services of all who can work in this vast and difficult field. In vain will they develop vigor and power of body in the young, and brighten and quicken the intellect, if the cunning of the one, and the passions and appetites that spring from the other, be not held in subjection by the elevation and strengthening of the heart.

HELPERS IN THE WORK.

We offer to do a work for our own poor, which you yourselves confess you cannot accomplish. We possess, in our religious orders of Brothers and Sisters, armies of skilled teachers voluntarily consecrated to the work of laboring among poor children, and instructing them in secular learning, while grounding them in virtue and morality. They are ready to spend their lives in this work of highest love and self-sacrifice; they can reach the hearts of these children of poverty; they can calm turbulent passions, and teach self-restraint, love of order, and respect for the rights of others.

The large cities need the services of these workers and teachers. It is unwise, it is worse, to cast them off, in view of the non-success of common schools to reach thousands of poor children; it is unwise to assert principles, that, logically carried out, lead to communism; it is dangerous unto madness to hinder the influences of religion from reaching to the lanes and by-ways of our crowded cities; it is sowing discord, and engendering heart-burnings, to trample on the just rights of any class in a Republic.

Parental rights, involving parental duties imposed by the natural and the revealed law, sanctioned and upheld by the common law and the Constitution, cannot be persistently disregarded without danger and detriment to the nation.

FUNDAMENTAL PRINCIPLES.

In a few words let me resume and give some conclusions logically deducible from the facts, statements, and arguments submitted to you in this paper.

In a Republic whose citizens are of different religious beliefs, who are voters needing intelligence, who are parents breeding races of freemen, the following principles are primary and vital:

1. The non-interference of the State in religious matters, in church or in school.

2. Compulsory knowledge, through parents' schools, under parents' control, and at their cost.

3. Free trade in education, or no monopoly of the teacher's profession.

RELIGION IN SCHOOLS.*

The ill-considered rashness with which the old system of public education was discarded to make way for one new and untried, here or elsewhere, is beginning to torment its victims. Not every change is an improvement. But the spirit of unstableness and change is the spirit of our age and country. In the name of progress, change is demanded in religion and education, as in habits and fashion. Changes in religion have multiplied sects. Some call this a gain. Radical changes in methods of school management leave us to-day without instruction in the simplest truths of Christianity—without the most elementary code of morals, on a foundation of Christian authority. Moralists esteem this a loss.

So far has the experiment of eliminating religion from even primary schools been pushed, that these have become truly "Christless and Godless." This change is recent. It is only within a few years—within a generation—that the old methods of disciplining the young in morals and religion have been made to yield to the new ones resting on expediency, good manners, and supposed worldly advantage. The beginnings of the change were gradual; within the last ten years advocates of the exclusion of all religious teaching have been loud, urgent, imperative and successful. The demand to secularize education admits of no question. It is a curious fact, but not the less true, that the American people have been trained down to this low standard by

---
*This article appeared originally in the North American *Review* for April, 1881, and is here republished with permission.

the very ministers who now clamor for a return to the old ways. A hearing on the merits of the question that would not have been conceded yesterday, can be had to-day, because thoughtful men, not ministers or politicians, amazed and disappointed at the firstfruits of the common schools, after years of trial and lavish expenditures of money, anxiously ponder over and seek light upon the moral and social problem of the future of our children in cities and towns. These fair-minded men ask, and, by the necessities of the hour, they are justified in asking, Can a republic, of all forms of government, endure, whose children, for generations, are educated in schools without religion, without God?

To understand the character and extent of the change which has come over our system of schools, and to show the moorings from which it has broken loose, and the rock on which it has stranded, it is worth while to examine the early history of the establishment of public schools in the State of New York. What is true of this State is, in some degree, true of all the States. The founders of the public-school system were men strongly imbued with religious ideas, and profound reverence for God's law, as they found and understood it in the Bible. State constitutions assumed that the people were Christians, and that their children should be educated as Christians. Virtue, morality, and religion were claimed as essential to the existence of a republican form of government. So long as the American people remained evangelically Protestant in church forms and belief, public schools were conducted as schools biblically Protestant. A large infusion of religious teaching and influence pervaded them. And thus the parents, the children, the teachers, and the public officials were in accord, and the virtue and morality contemplated by the State constitutions, and deemed in the highest degree essential to the bringing up of law-abiding citizens, were secured.

The first free school not in connection with a church society was founded in New York City in 1805. Its trustees issued an address, from which the following words are taken: " It is proposed, also, to establish, on the first day of the week, a school called a Sunday-School, more particularly for such children as, from peculiar circumstances, are unable to attend on the other days of the week. In this, as in the common school, it will be a primary object, without observing the peculiar forms of any religious society, to inculcate the sublime truths of religion and morality contained in the Holy Scriptures." After several years of work, its trustees, of whom DeWitt Clinton was president, published an address to the parents of the children in attendance on this school, in which this paragraph is found: " The trustees of the New York free school, however desirous they may be to promote the improvement of the scholars in school learning, to qualify and fit them for the common duties of life, cannot view with an eye of indifference the more primary object of an education calculated to form habits of virtue and industry, and to inculcate the general principles of Christianity," etc. When this Free School Society was, in 1825, merged in the Public School Society, the same leading idea of a morality based on Scriptural teachings was continued. In pursuing this course, the managers were in harmony with popular sentiment and the religious views of the vast majority of their patrons. Indeed, the non-Catholic church schools ceased to be necessary, and were for the most part abandoned. The new schools were satisfactory to non-Catholic religionists, whose prejudices, however, were so intense and blinding that they failed to understand why Catholics were unwilling to accept what pleased them.

The ideas prevailing in Massachusetts, Connecticut, Vermont, New Hampshire, and New York, on the subject of the training and education of the young, found their way into the constitutions and school statutes of the new States of the West. The Bill of Rights of Ohio is a fair sample of all. Its third section reads: " Religion, morality, and knowledge being essentially necessary to good government and the happiness of mankind, schools and the means of instruction shall forever be encouraged by legislative provision not inconsistent with the rights of conscience." This was not intended to be a fine phrase with which to adorn the statute-book. It meant that religion and morality should be imparted to children in State schools hour by hour, with instruction in all branches of needful secular knowledge, by teachers of correct morals and Christian belief. It was furthermore strictly enjoined that great care should be used in the selection of Christian teachers.

In thus prescribing a plan for the management of schools, these early evangelical Christians, and the political States whose constitutions and statutes they molded and shaped, showed remarkable harmony with the prescriptions of the Catholic Church on the same subject. It is an incontrovertible fact that the founders of the American Republic believed that religion could not with safety be divorced from secular education, and of necessity ordained that the tone, ideas, and practices familiar to parents in churches should be conserved in the schools to which they intrusted their children.

In consonance with the same idea, the Catholic Church holds that the religion which is good for parents in the Church ought to be good for their children in the school, and in what is known as the Syllabus, expresses her mind on this subject. She condemns as an error the following proposition: " Catholics may approve of a plan of education withdrawn from Catholic faith and the authority of the Church, and which concerns itself only with natural sciences, and the worldly ends of social life, solely, or, at least, primarily." Just as evangelical Protestants hold that religious knowledge should accompany secular learning in schools for evangelical children, so Catholics claim, in full accord with the Syllabus, that Catholic children should be indoctrinated in the teachings of the Bible by teachers of the same faith as their fathers; and, furthermore, since virtue, to become habitual, needs practice and daily use, they claim that their children should be made familiar with the observances and duties ordained by Christ, and always preserved and enforced in the Catholic Church.

That the truth and wisdom of the Syllabus are appreciated by non-Catholics, may be learned from what follows.

In 1869, the Rt. Rev. A. Cleveland Coxe published "Moral Reforms," a book made up of pastoral letters addressed at various times to members of his church. In instructing his communicants, he seems to catch the very spirit of the Syllabus, and thus gives three rules for their spiritual guidance:

"1. Secure to every human being the very best education you can provide for him.

"2. When you can do no better, utilize the common schools, and supplement them by all additional means of doing good.

"3. But where we can do better, let us do our full duty to our own children, and to all children, by gathering them into schools and colleges thoroughly Christian."

In thus explicitly laying down the law, Bishop Coxe interprets correctly the mind of the Protestant Episcopal denomination. In a General Convention held in New York City, the following resolution was adopted: "*Resolved*, That the bishops and clergy be most earnestly requested to bring this subject to the attention of the members of this Church, that they remind the people of their duty to support our own schools and colleges, and to make education under the auspices of the Protestant Episcopal Church superior in all respects to that which is afforded in other institutions."

The Presbyterians, in General Assembly, " recommend their congregations to establish primary and other schools, on the plan of teaching the truths and duties of our holy religion in connection with the useful branches of secular learning." In the same sense, all classes of evangelical religionists speak out from time to time. Now, it is the Congregationalists in the "Advance," of Chicago; then it is the editor of the "Methodist," the chief organ of the Methodists. The latter, in an editorial, says: "Again, a firm and genial Christian tone pervading a school, by warming the heart, stimulating conscience, and strengthening and bracing up all the better elements of one's nature, is eminently calculated to predispose the pupil to faith as well as to virtue." But of all denominations, the Baptists have put themselves on record as most decidedly opposed to schools from which religious teaching and influences have been excluded. It is certainly gratifying to

Catholics to know that Protestants, in reality, agree with them regarding the necessity of religious teachings and observances in children's schools, even if they do not live up to their belief. Many of the secular newspapers re-echo the language of the pulpit. Notable among them is the " Journal of Commerce," of New York City.

But after such strong expressions on the part of State Legislatures in the past, and on the part of conventions and assemblies to-day, what are the rights of religion in State schools, in the year of the Lord 1881 ? New York State has made as great progress in the eliminating of every shade and semblance of religious instruction and usages from its common schools as any other State in the Union. The ruling of its department of public instruction is precise and peremptory. Mr. Randall, in making known decisions of his predecessors in the office of superintendent of public schools, uses this language : "In view of the above facts, the position was early, distinctly, and almost universally taken by our statesmen, legislators, and prominent friends of education—men of the warmest religious zeal, and belonging to every sect—that religious education must be banished from the public schools, and consigned to the family and the church. * * * We have seen that even prayer—that morning and evening duty which man owes to his Creator, * * * has been decided by two of our most eminent superintendents as inadmissible as a school exercise within school hours, and that no pupil's conscience or inclination shall be violated by being compelled to listen to it." When Bishop Coxe asks that the Bible shall not be excluded from State schools, it is evident he is not aware of these rulings of competent authority.

The above is the law for the State of New York. The city has a special law by which the reading of the Bible is retained in its schools. In many State schools the Bible is still read, in a very perfunctory way, it is true, but any dissentient has only to demand its exclusion to be gratified, for under the above law the Bible has no place in a State school. The custom adopted in some schools, of keeping young children, not criminals, shivering on the cold side of a door while Bible-reading is going on within the school-room, or the substitute gravely suggested by a high dignitary, of inflicting on the helpless innocents "the listening to the reading of State constitutions and sundry municipal laws," may be commendable for nicety of persecution, and as a refinement on past methods, but it is out of place in America. The clauses in the constitutions guaranteeing civil and religious liberty would elicit curious comments from the young martyrs, freezing and tortured for conscience sake. The American people will not tolerate unnecessary mental suffering of children because their elders cannot agree on a system of schools adapted to the moral and intellectual needs of all classes. It is not the children's fault that American Christians are divided into numberless sects, "working out into manifold abuses, rivalries, and even conflicts."

It has been shown what is the teaching of the Catholic Church with regard to the exclusion of religion from schools ; it has also been demonstrated by the utterances of the highest authority in several Protestant denominations, how great is the agreement between them and Catholics. It is proper now to note how these two bodies accept the decision of political authorities by which every tittle of religious instruction is excluded from school-rooms. When Catholics proposed a compromise with evangelical Christians by which equal rights might be secured to all without the sacrifice of an inestimable blessing, a majority of their non-Catholic fellow-citizens confronted them with angry looks and fierce determination to listen to no reasonable remonstrance, even, but to enforce unrelentingly the establishment of free schools all over the State, in which neither prayer nor the Bible should be tolerated. The uselessness of contending against an overpowering majority, not in the best humor, on a question that had found its way into the arena of politics, was soon apparent. With sadness of soul they gave up the attempt to arrange with their fellow-citizens a system of schools, that, securing universal education, might do so without sacrificing essential principles, and without disregarding most sacred rights of parents and children. Between Catholics on one side and evangelicals on the other, infidels, agnostics, secularists, and Jews stepped in and captured the field.

To Catholics it became clear that if they meant to transmit the faith of their baptism to their offspring, if they believed that Christ's religion was worth living for, if they held that God should not be driven out of the school-house, and that the virtue, morality, and religion essential to a republican form of government were to be perpetuated, they would have to establish a system of schools for their own children, under their control, and at their cost. The outlook, from a temporal point of view, was forbidding, and, except to men of the martyr spirit, without a ray of hope along the horizon. Crowds of poor immigrants flocking to our shores for shelter from oppression and the miseries of the Old World, intent on finding a patch of ground and a roof as a home, had no treasures to offer for the erection of educational buildings. And, even if the buildings were up and ready for occupancy, whence should come the army of skilled instructors, with God and the love of God's little one's in their hearts, to undertake, on a sudden, the training of these thousands of the poor of Christ? But, the time for words and discussion having passed, that for action and work had come. As the cause was God's, Catholics put their trust in Him.

Abandoning all hope of help from their fellow-citizens, Catholics are now providing satisfactory schooling for their children all over the country. What Bishop Coxe and the Convention of Protestant Episcopal Bishops entreat their followers to procure for the children of their church members, has been placed within the reach of the poorest member of the Catholic Church. The irreligious and secular world will judge religionists by their deeds, rather than by resolutions and rhetorical speeches at conventions. In some sections of the country, in Massachusetts, for example Catholics have held back from establishing Catholic schools in the hope that their neighbors, the majority, would listen to reason and agree upon a plan by which all classes of citizens might be secured in their rights. These hopeful people are losing hope. The ministers and the politicians will not permit the people to exercise their common sense and act in accordance with their natural impulses of justice and fair play.

To understand the amount of educational work accomplished by the Catholics of the United States, a few statistics will be useful. According to "Sadlier's Directory" for 1881, there were in Christian free schools, of a grade corresponding with the common or State schools, 423,383 children, whose education in State schools would have required $6,164,456.16, computing the cost at the average per scholar estimated by the Commissioner of Education for 1878—a large annual saving in favor of non-Catholic tax-payers. New York State had 270 Christian free schools, attended by 80,429 pupils.

In New York city there are fifty-seven Catholic churches under the care of resident pastors. Of these parishes thirty-two have Christian free schools. Special reports for 1880 have been received from twenty-three of these parishes. They had an average attendance of 21,550 scholars. The great majority of the teachers were brothers and sisters of different religious orders. The amount paid for tuition alone was $100,928.16; for books, $8,638.93; for janitors, $8,397.00; for sundry expenses, coal, repairs, etc., $27,147.50. The estimated value of these twenty-three school-buildings, including ground and furniture, is placed at $1,501,300.00, omitting the cost of residences for teachers. As tax-payers in New York City pay for tuition at the rate of $20.30 for each child in its grammar and primary schools, they are saved $437,465.00 annually by these twenty-three Christian free schools. In a few years the parishes whose school-buildings are insufficient to receive all children whose spiritual care is on the conscience of the pastor, will have erected larger ones; and the other parishes not yet provided with these necessary school-churches for children, because of heavy indebtedness incurred in erecting expensive churches for parents, and because in some neighborhoods fine music is held of more account than the care of the young, will also have joined their sister parishes in a noble rivalry to work with whole-heartedness, as the Syllabus and the Church teach, in gathering into Christian schools, from which the great thought of the life to come is not excluded, all the children of the flock. Priests and people who do not believe as the Church teaches have lost the faith. Priests and people who fail to live up to their faith because of heavy sacrifices to be made are unworthy of membership in a Church that demands of her disciples heroic sacrifices to preserve the faith. It is then only a question of time when there will be ample school room in every Catholic parish of New York City for all children having a right to a Christian education.

As the above figures refer to schools in the great metropolis, others, relating to a much smaller city and in the rural districts, may be of interest. In Rochester there are eleven parishes, ten of which have Christian schools. In these there was, in 1880, an average attendance of 4391 scholars. To teachers the amount paid was $14,152.39. As it cost the tax payers of Rochester, in 1879, $117,387.57 to pay teachers for 8017 children, or at the rate of $14.64 per scholar, simple arithmetic tells us that the 4391 scholars in Christian free schools saved non-Catholic tax-payers $64,284.24 for teachers, not to speak of additional expenses for buildings, coal, repairs, etc. Catholic school-houses in Rochester are valued at $250,000. It is a costly price to pay for religion's sake, but it is well worth this, and more!

We turn now to our non-Catholic friends, believers in Christianity, and ask, What have you done for the religious and moral education of your young? It is well known that educational establishments for the wealthier members of your flocks, in which religious and secular education are combined, are worthy of all praise, and bespeak the zeal of ministers and the liberality of laymen; but what have you accomplished for the poor children of your denomination, in view of the utter failure of the public schools? How have your congregations responded to the admonitions and entreaties of the General Assembly and the Protestant Episcopal Convention?

The weakest suggestion of a reform is the demand to replace the Bible in the public schools. The uselessness of the Bible as a mere reading-book was demonstrated long ago. As a teacher of morals and religion, it needed the living voice of a competent instructor to explain its meaning and enforce its authority and precepts, thus turning the school into a church. As a sign of antagonism to Catholics, it has ceased to play a part, for Catholics are no longer there to note the intended insult, or to heed the fumbling and crumpling of its pages by irreverent scholars. Bible-reading that teaches no dogma to children's minds is like trying to feed their bodies with dry husks. Theology without dogma may be adapted to the "Church of the Future," of which the agnostics are preparing to be the high-priests, but it is now an unknown quantity.

It is profound reverence for the Bible which induces Catholics to object to it in schools as an ordinary reading-book. Yet more do they object to its use in the hearing of their children when the teacher is one whose sympathies and belief are opposed to their faith. The school-master may never speak a word adverse to Catholic doctrine, and yet exercise a pernicious influence over the minds and hearts of Catholic children. The power of personality in the teacher is strongly placed before his hearers by the Rev. Dr. Hall, Presbyterian minister in New York City. In a Sunday sermon he says: "You cannot detach absolutely the person of the teacher from the thing taught. One may ask, What can religion have to do with algebra? Now, if you could get teaching without personal influence, that might be true. But you cannot," etc. Earnest and devout Christians see that much of the growing contempt for the Sacred Scriptures is due to unwise and indiscriminate reading by young school-children, whose attention is called to passages suggestive of evil by perverted companions, or to its cold, hesitating, half-hearted, mechan ical reading by skeptical masters. Personal influence is often more active and seductive on the play-ground than in the school-room. Catholics desire the exclusion of the Bible and of religion from schools to which, for the time being, they are compelled to send their children, in default of schools of their own. They grieve to see the exultation of secularists and infidels over the easy victory evangelicals have permitted them to win. The secularists, not Catholics, wave aloft the banner of triumph.

It will require a stronger argument than imputed lack of patriotism on the part of Catholics to re-introduce the Bible into the public schools, such as is offered by Bishop Coxe. This stale and decrepit calumny raises a blush on the cheeks of some, and flashes fire from the eyes of others. It may do for the hustings on voting day, but it is unworthy of attention from serious and just men, who know the historical record of Catholics on every battle field from 1776 to 1865.

Such a cruel innuendo could be thrown out only by one who wrote of "Romanists:" "Their arithmetic is wonderful, and their moral theology concerning oaths allows the widest exercise of imagination in making out returns and reports."* The writer of this sentence would be barred as a juror in any court of Christendom, were this question on trial. The country is full of American Catholic citizens who smile at inane distinctions in their membership, kindly suggested by non-Catholic friends. These Catholics, so loyal and so true, may fearlessly challenge comparison with their maligners in all that proves devotedness and fidelity to the country and the constitution.

The taunt that when Catholics become the majority they will not tolerate others, may be relegated to the same category of popular claptrap good for electioneering times, but not to be flung out when men are seriously discussing how best to secure the stability of our common country. Should Catholics at any time, and in any part of the country, grow to be the majority,

---

*"Moral Reforms," by A. Cleveland Coxe.

they will take delight in placing the minority on a footing of equality with themselves, even as the French Canadians, forty years ago, being then a large majority of the inhabitants of Lower Canada, settled this question of schools, in its moral and religious aspect, by conceding to the Protestant minority every privilege and claim asked for. It is an unfortunate suggestion to offer that to keep Catholics from practicing intolerance toward a Protestant minority, it is advisable for a Protestant majority to be intolerant toward a Catholic minority.

The belief is growing day by day that the public schools, as now constituted, are failures. Richard Grant White cries aloud only what is in many minds. It is distressing to be obliged to admit that the idol of our national worship is a false god; that education in earthly things, solely or primarily, does not make good citizens; that unbounded expenditures of money bring no adequate return; that the very principle of State pupilage is radically defective, and worse, is highly dangerous, fostering, as it does, the most cankerous social and political evil of the age—Communism. It demands renewed efforts on the part of teachers and superintendents, paid officials of the schools, to keep the people from seeing these truths.

When the people of New York state were cajoled into the free-school system, with its denial of parental control, the promise was held out to the anxious tax-payers that increased taxation for schools would be followed by lessened taxation for alms-houses, prisons, and lunatic asylums. The former will cost less, so said partisans of the new system. Has the promise been kept? Our educated rogues are shrewder, and escape with greater facility from the meshes and restraints of the law, but our houses of correction are multiplying out of all proportion to increase of population; and lunatic asylums, State and county, cannot keep pace in number and accommodation with the demand made on them by victims of shattered brains and morals. The increase of crimes, not alone of crimes which send their perpetrators to jail, but of crimes which destroy the fountain of life, and the startingly progressive multiplication of divorces destroying all hope of Christian families, the prop and mainstay of a republic, alarm ministers and laymen, and justify the verdict of "Failure." Schools that won sympathy on the plea of providing a plain education for plain people have spread out into high schools, academies, colleges and universities. Normal schools give a professional training to young men and women who, for the most part, have no thought of following a teacher's career, for the compensation usually given is not commensurate with their expectations. Notwithstanding unlimited expenditures of public money, complaint is heard that instruction in the elementary branches of learning falls short of what the people have a right to expect, and "Failure" is written again.

But when in large cities, such as New York and Rochester, a third of the children turn from the open door of the public school, on conscientious grounds, and seek schooling in other buildings, put up and paid for by citizens the least able to open their slim purses to a second tax-gathering, it becomes a duty to proclaim the existing system a "failure," and a cruel wrong. The "failure" is more evident when separate schools are needed for colored children, banned for the accident of color. It is yet more marked when the system requires poor schools, under the Children's Aid Society, to make room for those who suffer from the misfortune of poverty. But when a system of free schools, that seventy-five years ago began an assault on private and church schools for the alleged reason that there are some few children uncared for, and monopolized the teacher's work and profession by the power of the general treasury, to-day has to admit that there are adrift and untaught in the streets of one city from ten to twenty thousand children of the very class in whose behalf State charity finds its justification, acknowledgment of "failure" becomes more than a necessity.

By way of help to a return to correct principles and methods, some truths are here indicated:

First. We forgot Amerian traditions when religion was driven out of the schools.

Second. We forgot them when the State was allowed to step in between the father and his child.

Third. We forgot them when we imported European ideas of paternal government, and began the breeding of communistic social heresies.

Fourth. No nation, not Christian in belief and morals, can flourish in our civilization.

Fifth. Virtue and morality, to become a habit of life, need the teaching and disciplining of the school, as well as of the church and family.

Sixth. Knowledge does not lessen vice. Will and conscience, helped by God's law and grace, restrain passions and evil inclinations.

Seventh. Since the State has no religion, and cannot teach morals on the authority of Divine truth, its incapacity to educate is beyond doubt.

The sooner we return to sound principles, the same on which the founders of the Republic built and prospered, the easier will it be to repair the mischief of the last few years, and the greater and more reasonable will be the hope of the stability of our institutions. If our people were one in religious belief and worship, the question of schools would present no difficulty. The only obstacle to a just and righteous settlement is the unwillingness of the majority to concede to the minority rights that are heaven-born, that are the very life of a republican form of government, and that guard and uphold the consciences of every class in the community.

RELIGIOUS TEACHING IN SCHOOLS.*

The system of state schools, or public or common schools, is a subject of interesting and profitable discussion. The temper in which it is carried on to-day is an improvement on the methods of fifty years ago. The change from the violent and domineering style once common, now rare, gives hope of an ultimate and satisfactory settlement. The interests at stake are too momentous for the Republic's welfare and peace, as well as for the just rights of millions of its citizens, to be left much longer in abeyance. Besides, the number of just-minded and reasonable Americans is rapidly increasing. With the dying out of the senseless bigotry of a past generation, the atmosphere is purified of thick and unhealthy vapors disturbing to mind and soul.

In 1840, William H. Seward and John C. Spencer, leaders in the old Whig Party but statesmen far in advance of the times, proposed an equitable arrangement for the conduct of schools, by which the fair wishes and demands of the state, of religious and secular corporations, and of individuals should be fully heeded and subserved. They proceeded on the supposition that the main object in view was the education of the children of the people on the broadest and most just basis, and without the erection of barriers for the exclusion of masses of children greatly needing help. The excitement which ensued showed the uselessness of discussion during a tempest of unreasoning, invective and angry passions. The moment for argument had not come.

---
*This article appeared originally in the *Forum* of December, 1889, and is here republished with permission.

During the summer of the present year two conventions met, One, the assembly of school teachers, held its session at Nashville; the other, a gathering of clergymen for the most part, and belonging in tone of thought to a generation of fifty years ago congregated at Saratoga. The Nashville convention invited two eminent Catholic ecclesiastics to address its body. Their papers on the need and advantage of religious instruction in the schools were listened to with attention and respect. The Saratoga convention proved, to the shame of civil and religious liberty, that the age of persecution for the sake of conscience had not passed. The sentiments to which its members, lay and cleric, gave expression, in speech and resolutions, are annoying to law-abiding citizens, but harmless, because inoperative, dead. Their desire to rivet a wrong and to perpetuate a deplorable injustice, is made manifest. No discussion is possible with such men. A few years more will see the extinction of the race.

To come to an understanding as to a system of school education that will answer the requirements of the state without sacrificing the just rights of individuals, the points of agreement and divergence should be carefully considered. Roman Catholics and Evangelicals of all denominations (and they are the vast majority of our population) hold that their children should receive a religious education and training. There is satisfactory unanimity of sentiment on this point. The divergence begins with regard to the amount of this religious instruction, the basis on which it should be given, and the place in which it should be imparted. Catholics maintain that, conjointly and in harmony with religious teaching in the family and the church, there should be regular lessons in religion in the every-day school; that these lessons should be on a doctrinal basis, and to the extent of a child's capacity to absorb a daily lesson in religious truths. Less important subjects in secular learning require daily study and explanation. Evangelical Christians are divided in sentiment. Protestant Episcopalians hold, as Bishop Coxe, of Western New York, testifies, that "they should do their full duty to their children by gathering them into schools and colleges thoroughly Christian." The establishment and maintenance of academies and colleges by Episcopalians for the thoroughly Christian education of their children, verifies the correctness of the Bishop's statement. Presbyterians in their general assemblies, and Baptists and Methodists in conferences and synods, are equally explicit on this question. These various ecclesiastical bodies illustrate the sincerity of their public utterances, so far as the education of the children of their wealthy members is concerned; they fail lamentably when the education of the children of their poorer co-religionists is in question. Rev. Dr. Kendrick, in the *Forum* for September, concedes that "morality cannot be inculcated in the most effective manner without religious enforcements;" and yet, when Catholics, in schools of their own, because there is no place for them in state schools, choose to educate their children where morality can be most effectively inculcated with the help of "religious enforcements," he pronounces their choice a luxury, for the enjoyment of which they ought to be mulcted.

There are men to-day who lose their wits when the specter of Jesuitism or Romanism dances before their affrighted imaginations. It is hard to reason with these disturbed but well-meaning gentlemen. They speak and write of Italy and Ireland, when others are studying American problems; they write of "dumping" European criminals on American shores, when serious men are planning how best to keep down the breeding of criminals in our large cities; they picture the Pope in the supposed act of nullifying our national laws, when citizens to the manner born ask that our laws shall not ride rough-shod over parental and conscientious rights. It is hard to carry on reasonable discussion with men sure of their personal infallibility; with men whose thoughts and ideas are warped by the battle cries of fifty years ago. Thoughtful men do not to-day fall down before the state school system as before a fetich to be blindly worshiped. It is a system of schools thoroughly Godless, in name and in law, established and maintained by the state for the secular education of the children of the people who are satisfied with a partial, ineffective, and unjust arrangement, and who are willing to accept pecuniary aid from poor neighbors for their offspring's schooling. Catholics are unceasingly hectored about their attempts to overthrow and destroy the state school system. Attention is thus drawn away from real dangers altogether inherent in the system itself. It is a system liable to blunders innumerable, to insufficiency of accomplishment, and to the perpetrating of injustices. Any blunder in the system that deprives a notable number of children of its advantages, defeats the end of its existence; any radical principle essentially faulty in its nature, becomes a source of mischief and danger; any part of its working machinery that rasps the just rights of others, will one day throw the whole establishment into confusion ending in ruin.

1. There are at the present time considerably more than 600,000 Catholic children in the parochial schools of the United States. Surely this can be called a notable number. The parents of these children are unwilling to deprive their offspring of an effective Christian education. They prove the sincerity of their convictions by bearing patiently with the sacrifices they are called on to make, and revel in the "luxury" of suffering for the sake of conscience. It is an aggravation of the wrong done them to question their earnestness and sincerity.

2. A radical principle underlying the state school system is its unadulterated communism. The assertion that the state has the right to educate at the common expense one class of children to the practical exclusion of another class, is communism in its worst form. Every argument adduced to justify it in relieving parents, in one line of duty, of burdens they are able to carry, may be brought forward to relieve them in other lines of duty. It is the duty of a father, who is not a pauper, to feed, to clothe, to shelter, and to educate his children. The state, in the name of humanity, does for parents only what they are unable to do for themselves. Chicago people are as logical as Herbert Spencer, and deduce from the principle of state schoolism the justification

of state tailorism. Children in Chicago who plead that they cannot go to school for want of suitable clothing, are supplied by that city of socialistic tendencies with state trousers, frocks, and shoes. Herbert Spencer, in "Social Statics," argues:

"If the benefit, importance, or necessity of education be assigned as a sufficient reason why government should educate, then may the benefit, importance, or necessity of food, clothing, shelter, and warmth be assigned as a sufficient reason why government should administer these also."

When parental responsibility abdicates in favor of governmental responsibility, encouragement is lent to mendicancy, and the breeding of pauperism begins. Shutting our eyes to this unwelcome truth does not make it less a truth. Having drifted away from the sound practices of our American forefathers, who believed in paying for the education, secular and religious, of their children, we find ourselves swept along in a flood of pernicious political principles.

3. Another radical defect in the system of state schools, is that it takes a poor man's hard-earned dollars to help richer neighbors provide their children with an education that will fit them for their life work, for college, for a profession. The state school has ceased to be a school for an elementary education. There was a time when friends of state schools had much to say about the Republic's need of an elementary education for the children of the masses. It is a mockery of the truth to talk, in these days, of an elementary education in any of our cities or towns. The system embraces everything from a kindergarten to a college. It needs only two other provisions to be perfect—a nursery for babes and a university for the state's pauperized pets. Kindergartens are for children too young to go to school, but troublesome to keep in the house, whose parents are willing to be relieved of maternal and home cares for a few hours in the day, at the expense of the state. Why not provide cradles, baby wagons, and attendants? Advocates of state paternalism run mad, such as Edward Bellamy, call for the highest curriculum of

studies up to eighteen and twenty years of age, and "a sufficient state provision for the support of the children of indigent parents while at school."*

The original and primary danger to the state school system is found, then, not in the assaults of any class in the community, but in its own manifold and inherent defects. Catholics are not antagonizing it; they are leaving it severely alone. They do not abuse its teachers or their pupils. Catholics know, especially here in Rochester, that its teachers are most estimable ladies and gentlemen, and that the pupils of the state schools are no worse than other children whose religious training is relegated to an hour's Sunday-school instruction, while arithmetic and spelling get five hours in a week. Evangelicals, in despair of ever making the system of state schools religious in their sense, hopelessly abandon it to the care of the sects of secularists, Ingersollists, and open and avowed infidels, while concentrating all their energies and pecuniary resources on academies and colleges for the education of the children of their rich parishioners. Catholics and German Lutherans are the only believers in Christianity who are logical and consistent. These have convictions and they live up to them, even if in doing so they have to spend money. They are not counted among the rich in this world's goods. Yet a venerable Christian minister of the gospel declares that when this gospel, which Christ said was to be preached to the poor, who had the first right to it, was to be taught in the school-room, it was a "luxury" for indulgence in which the poor were to be made to pay. Christ's teachings and men's do not always run in the same channel. Catholics are not complaining. It is easier, far easier, to suffer a wrong than to persecute. They ask to be left in peace. They are willing to pay with their own money for the "luxury" of religious teaching which their children enjoy. It is the wrong-doers, they who take poor people's money for their personal gain, who keep up disturbing and angry lamenta-

---
*See the Nationalist for July, 1889.

tions. A coachman pays for the schooling of his own boys; he helps educate in state schools his master's children. Is it any wonder that the questionings, answers, and comments that follow, throw the state school system out of gear? As an instance, it may be stated that here in Rochester, during the past summer months, neighbors' boys, Catholic and Evangelical, were playing together, as rightly they might. After their play they entered into a discussion of great social and economic questions not unworthy the consideration of eminent statesmen. A Catholic boy informed his evangelical playmate, a pupil in a state school, that while his Catholic father helped pay the other's tuition, the latter paid nothing for the Catholic boy's education. With the natural impulse of a warm-hearted and generous youth, the lad repelled the imputation on his and his father's sense of honor and justice, and appealed to the Catholic boy's father, a lawyer, to contradict his son's charge, for in his honest heart it did not seem possible that such a gross wrong could be perpetrated. The party adjourned to the lawyer's house and submitted the case. When the truth without exaggeration was made clear to the fair-minded boy, that he was the recipient of another boy's charity through his father, he was abashed and hung his head for very shame. So it will be with coming generations, who will listen to no silly twaddle about Ireland, Italy, and Spain, about the Pope, the Inquisition, and danger to our liberties. An American inquisition, persecuting by legal pecuniary taxation, will be more hateful in their eyes than any that history tells of, for this last form will have a flimsy covering of sham and hypocrisy for a cloak.

It may be said in reply that the whole amount of taxes paid into the common treasury by Catholics, is, owing to their poverty, too trifling to be noticed. Here is opened up the significant question of taxation. Consumers are the chief tax-payers. When the city or state swells the tax roll for increased schools and teachers, the landlord, the baker, the butcher, the dry-goods man distribute a portion of the increase on tenants and consumers. In western cities, where clerks, mechanics, and laborers own their dwellings, a direct tax is paid on the real estate, and an indirect tax through others, who, from the goods they sell to their customers, derive a share of the taxes they pay. This tax money is called state money. The state collects and distributes it. It is still the people's money. A man's rights go where his money goes. Much of this money is used for the maintenance of schools from which a large minority of citizens is barred out by disenabling conditions, arbitrary, illogical, and punitive.

There is another aspect of the case which renders a Catholic's hardship not quite as unbearable as at first sight it appears, while for non-Catholics who use the state schools the injustice done to the former is grosser and more apparent. Again I shall introduce Rochester to illustrate my point.

The last printed report of the Rochester public schools is for 1887–88. Their pupils numbered 12,302. For the same period the parochial schools counted 5,849, or more than 47½ per cent. of the number in the state schools. The total city tax levy for 1887 was $1,254,239, of which $252,00 was for the schools—or nearly 21 per cent. of the general city taxes was for the schooling of its specially-favored 12,302 children. Hence, were the Catholics to disband their parochial schools, and throw their 5,849 children on the city, school taxes would have to be increased more than 47½ per cent., or more than $119,600, without counting the cost of the fourteen or fifteen new school-houses, together with lots on which to build them, furniture, etc. If any Catholic or non-Catholic taxpayer of Rochester wishes to know how much is saved to his pocket by the maintenance of parochial schools, let him take his city tax bill, divide it by five, and he will have a little less than the amount which he pays for educating the children now in its state schools. If he then add 48 per cent. to this amount, he will have what he would be obliged to pay were our children, now in parochial schools, educated in state schools, at the same proportionate expense. In other words, the non-Catholic tax-payer saves 48 per cent. of one-fifth of his entire tax bill, that is, nearly one-tenth of it; and the Catholic tax-payer saves the same amount, less what he contributes to the support of his parochial school. Is it any wonder, then, that Catholics are not fretting or worrying over the absence of their children from state schools? The injustice inflicted on them by those who take Catholic money for state schools is, however, none the less grievous.

The pretext for this punishment is that our schools are sectarian. Heaven bless the mark! And what are theirs? It is a cry as senseless as a mischievous school boy's cry of "mad dog" on a crowded street. It strikes terror and scatters the timorous. Sensible men know that sectarianism is a two-edged sword; it cuts more ways than one. In the New York constitutional convention of 1866, it was proposed to submit to the people an amendment prohibiting all help to sectarian institutions. The sense in which "sectarian" would be understood by learned judges in the last court of appeal being pointed out by some of the shrewder members of the convention, the subject was quietly dropped. If it could be construed to mean only "Romanism" and "Romanists," all would work well; but should it appear to carry the meaning given to it by John C. Spencer, secretary of State and superintendent of public instruction, there was danger of such an amendment hurting more than Romanists. Secretary Spencer, in his report to the New York Legislature of 1841, wrote:

"Religious doctrines of vital interest will be inculcated, not as theological exercises, but incidentally in the course of literary and scientific instruction; and who will undertake to prohibit such instruction? * * * It is believed to be an error to suppose that the absence of all religious instruction, if it were practicable, is a mode of avoiding sectarianism. On the contrary, it would be in itself sectarian; because it would be consonant to the views of a particular class, and opposed to the opinions of other classes."

Secretary Spencer secures listeners where Catholics can get no hearing. The sectarianism of Ingersoll, of Secularists, of

Agnostics, of Evangelicals, is repugnant to Catholics; but they loathe with supreme contempt the sectarianism of those who pretend that their particular development of sectarianism, their views, their opinions, are so milk-and-watery (the power for good as a religious force being washed out of them) that they ought to be acceptable to all other sectarians. It is hard for Catholics to believe in the sincerity of men who put forward this silliness about sectarianism. By what right does the state hand over one dollar of Catholic money to maintain sectarian schools of the Ingersoll, the secularistic, the avowed infidel, or the evangelical type, while it refuses to give back to Catholics, for their so-called sectarian schools, a portion of their own money?

Rev. Dr. Kendrick laments that his fellow citizens of Poughkeepsie have a correct sense of justice, and desire to deal fairly with their Catholic townspeople. It is greatly to their credit. They are not, however, the first in the country to rise above the bigotry of former days. Indeed, there are many towns and villages in this and other States where the same honest fairness has been observed for many years past, with even broader views of justice and a kindlier spirit. Still, many Catholics doubt the advisability of the "Poughkeepsie plan." It has advantages and disadvantages. It smacks of a union of state and church which in a country like ours is not desirable. To some degree it weakens and deadens the Catholicity of our school-rooms. Because, forsooth, Catholics who have leased to the state, school buildings, for use during the allotted daily school hours, choose before and after such hours to occupy them, at their own expense, for lessons in religion—for those "religious enforcements" without which "morality cannot be effectively inculcated"—Rev. Dr. Kendrick is prompted to say:

"Five minutes, or one minute, before the stroke of the regular school bell, they [the school buildings] may be the scene of religious exercises such as are not simply forbidden in the course of teaching prescribed by the state, but are actually offensive, in some of their features at least, to the vast majority of the American people. From lessons enforcing the worship of the Virgin Mary * * * the pupils pass—perhaps without breaking ranks, or special tokens of transition--to their secular lessons."

The same performance takes place in innumerable state schools, unavoidably frequented by Catholic children. Evangelical prayers, hymns, and Bible lessons are enjoyed, morality is effectively inculcated through "religious enforcements," and the pupils pass, without breaking ranks, to their secular lessons. Catholics do not complain, except when those of their children who have come a few minutes before the regular school hour, are kept waiting at the door in the rain, snow, and cold, while their school companions have the luxury of evangelical prayers and warmth within. What does the school of Dr. Kendrick want? Must our school buildings be put on a par with saloons on election day? No liquor can be sold within a certain distance of a polling booth. Shall it be enacted that God shall not be named, and no religious exercises be held, within a certain distance of a state school-house? When religious exercises can no longer be held within state school-houses, either before or after the hours for secular lessons, it will be time for Christians to abandon them to the sole use of infidels of every stripe. Then Sunday-school work will become inoperative, and empty churches and vacant pulpits will cover the land.

Rev. Dr. Kendrick again writes:

"When, however, we are confronted with the demand that the public school fund be split up and parceled out among the various churches, the spirit of concession should be replaced by the spirit of inflexible resistance."

Keeping in mind the scandals occasioned by the Bethel Baptist Church of New York City in 1820-21, which appropriated state school money for Baptist-church extension, the Doctor has cause for alarm. Catholics do not ask for a division of the school fund. Indeed, they fear the state. They ask simply for their own money, unjustly taken from them for the education of the children of infidels and Evangelicals. Be this amount much or little, it is theirs by every principle of common justice, and this, and not one dollar of any one else's money, they ask for. If this arrangement cannot be effected, then let the state pay for results in secular education, in any school, parochial, private, or corporate, furnishing the state with the requisite conditions of buildings, furniture, and competent and certificated teachers, and instructing pupils in such branches of secular learning as the state may require. If one or the other of these plans is not acceptable to the majority of the American people, then let us return to fundamental principles and throw the burden of schooling children on parents, where it rightly belongs. We ought by this time to see how dangerous it is to break away from sound principles in running democratic institutions.

Three objections are raised in opposition to the teaching of secular branches of learning in parochial schools, no matter how much inspection there may be on the part of the state: 1. These parochial schools fail to inspire their pupils with a patriotic love of country. 2. They are not up to the standard of state schools in secular learning. 3. They keep the children of a neighborhood from commingling one with another, and thus destroy the homogeneity—excuse the word—of the nation, something very desirable, so it is said.

It is hard to be called on to reply to the first objection. It is false and cruel. Only they who are inimical to Catholics on any and every pretense adduce it. Why are not some proofs furnished in sustainment of so wicked a calumny? A sufficient answer to this heartless aspersion on our honor as citizens, would be to invite these calumniators to visit our cemeteries and look on the tiny flags waving over the graves of patriots who died for their country's preservation. Members of the Grand Army of the Republic do not speak thus of their brothers in arms.

The second objection is equally false. It is not true that the standard of education in our parochial schools is not as high as that in state schools. In the city of Rochester both systems are well established, and are in fair and amicable competition. It is true that parochial schools are not victims to the vagaries of cranks. The latter are not permitted to run our schools, nor are these under the domination of school-book publishers. Nor are they "loaded down" with music, modern languages, the mechanical arts, savings banks, and military drill. They give that which they propose to give, a good elementary education. As an illustration of the truth of my contention, I cite what takes place in Rochester. Regents of the University of the State of New York send out to all schools, state, parochial, and private, that ask for them, sets of examination papers. The answers to these papers must have 75 per cent. of correctness in each branch of study. State school children are examined in their usual school buildings and before familiar teachers. Parochial school children are examined in the City High School and before strangers. The average age at which the latter graduate is fourteen years and two months; that at which the former graduate is over fifteen years. Another circumstance to be noted is the number entering the graduating class in September, and the number passing the regents' examination in June. In September of 1887, 18 entered the graduating class of the Cathedral School, and 22 that of the Immaculate Conception. All passed the examination in June, 1888. State school No. 4, in the same quarter of the city, had 28 in its graduating class at Christmas time, having already sifted out many that had entered it in September; and of these, only 18 stood the regents' test in June. We are not able to give the average number of points gained by the graduates of each school, as these are not published. What is accomplished in Rochester is a fair sample of successful results in other parochial schools of the State of New York. It may be asked, Why is the average age of the graduating pupils of the parochial schools so much lower than that of those in state schools? These children, for the most part of Irish and German parents, inherit sound and vigorous constitutions; they are not spoiled by injudicious and unhealthful feeding; they go to few night parties, if to any, and are consequently well rested in the morning, and fresh for another day's work; they have an object to work for, as they know that their future rests in large degree with themselves and the use they make of their early opportunities for study and self-advancement. No one will say that Celtic and Teutonic intellects are thick and slow of perception.

If our schools failed in secular studies, the blame could not be imputed to our teachers. These are mostly brothers and sisters who have consecrated their lives to educational work. With them it is a life work. Generally bright and intelligent when they enter a religious community, by daily study under competent teachers in normal schools, they prepare for the office of instructors. Their studies are kept up years after entrance into the school-room, under the guidance of the most capable of their body. There is no time lost in talking over the fashions; none in paying or receiving visits. Theatres and operas are not for them. Why should they not be, what they are, first-class teachers? Some members of these communities are sent abroad to acquire what there is worth knowing in European normal schools, together with a fluency in speaking foreign languages.

The flurry at Haverhill last spring, the agitation that ensued, and the disposition manifested by some to bring the power of the state to bear heavily on our work, serve an excellent purpose. They warn the superiors of convents that the teachers they send into the school-room must be thoroughly equipped in all that could by any possibility be demanded of them. In this sense the trials of the past will prove a blessing.

The third objection to parochial schools is that they hinder the commingling of the children of a neighborhood on the school playground, and thus fail to foster democratic equality. "Democratic equality" is a phrase with which to fool gudgeons. The wealthy of a town congregate in an aristocratic neighborhood, and right there will be found a state school, from which children of poverty will be, by force of circumstances, excluded. Thus the latter are deprived of social elevation through social commingling. Where this separation of rich and poor cannot be obtained in a district whose inhabitants are of both classes, the abolition of the recess removes all dangers of contact between the classes except in the class-room. It is in parochial schools that the democratic notion of friendly equality is best carried out. The religious brotherhood of man is taught and practically lived up to in these schools. We are ready for other objections, only let them contain a bit more of common sense.

The building of school-houses and the gathering into them of our Catholic children, are going bravely on all over the United States, especially in Massachusetts. Now that the Bostonians are fairly aroused, we may look to them for largeness and thoroughness of plans in educational achievement. They will accept, I am sure, no compromise by which the religious element in their daily tasks can be lessened. They will do their best to turn out good citizens and good Christians.

Catholics hold a proud position in the face of their fellow-citizens, though it is one for which they are heavily fined by state schoolism. In state schools: 1. Their parental rights and duties toward their children are infringed upon. 2. Their children's rights to a moral education and training by "religious enforcements" are seriously interfered with. 3. The natural dependence of children on parents is weakened. 4. The double taxation to which parents are subjected is irritating, unjust, and cruel; it is a hinderance to mutual esteem and to a kindly spirit among fellow-citizens. 5. They are made to suffer for the sake of conscience. It is not necessary to tell us again that somebody else's conscience ought to suit us.

It is, in some measure, compensation for our wrongs to be able to hold up our heads and to glory in our self-imposed sacrifices. It is ennobling to stand on a true American platform, and to enunciate principles such as the founders of our Republic knew and upheld. We believe in parental rights, and in the right of a child to a moral and religious training by the help of "religious enforcements;" we believe in all that tends to make a young man self-reliant and self-supporting; we believe in general education, as is shown by our school-houses honestly built, and their pupils honestly maintained, without a cent of help from the state; we believe that a truly religious man will be an upright and worthy citizen. We detest state paternalism and state pauperism.

Recent Utterances, of Which a Few are Here Given, Indicate a Marked Change in Public Sentiment on this Subject of State Schools and Christian Free Schools.

DR. JOHN BASCOM, in the *Forum* of March, 1891, says:
* * * Not only must the parochial school be sustained at the expense of those who establish it, but its supporters must also pay their proportion for the maintenance of the public schools, even when the work in their own school is accepted by the public as a just equivalent of its own work. This gives us, using language broadly, taxation without representation. The support of two sets of schools is thrown on the conscientious tax-payer, and he is told that his redress lies in giving up a method to which his convictions have led him.

* * * * * * * *

The underlying principle which sustains the public in its interference is thus covered up and lost sight of in the unfortunate circumstances of its application. This principle, that it may not bear the appearance of tyrannical intermeddling, should be accompanied by the principle that all instruction that is accepted in the place of public instruction shall have the same rights as public instruction. Those who are adequately educating their children under the inspection of the state should not be called upon to bear exactly the same burdens as if they were in neglect of this duty, or to render the duty twice over—once in a way conceded by the state and once in a way ordered by it. The intrinsic injustice of our existing policy has been concealed from us by the accidental, changeable and capricious impulses which have hitherto given rise to private schools, and by the fact that, for the most part, they have been established by the well-to-do simply in defense of class feeling. Now that the parochial schools express a religious conviction—no matter how mistaken that conviction may be—are closely and extendedly united with themselves, and are the chosen means of those who can ill endure a double expenditure, the bearings of this public policy are entirely altered. The sense of injustice will deepen year by year, the religious sentiments which underlie the parochial school will be fed by the very opposition which they meet, and the public feeling arrayed against these schools will itself become an intolerant sentiment, of belief or unbelief, associated with religion.

* * * * * * *

A large view of the objects to be gained, a wide, sympathetic grasp of existing conditions, and a clear sense of justice, will be able to find a way, and an ever-widening way, through present perplexities. Our public policy must show itself flexible—fully capable of freest adaptations. Bigotry may pertain to a too inflexible insistence on a method intrinsically desirable, as well as to a method in itself inadequate and narrow.

President ELIOT of Harvard at Boston College:

THE WHOLESOME VARIETY OF AMERICAN SCHOOLS.—The fourth of the entertainments under the patronage of the Young Men's Catholic Association of Boston College was given in the College Hall on Tuesday evening, January 19, being a lecture by Charles W. Eliot, LL.D., President of Harvard College, on "The Wholesome Variety of American Schools and Colleges." He was introduced by Thomas Mullen, President of the Association, and spoke in substance as follows:

I am to speak to you to-night of a subject which touches education and religion. I want to speak to you of the variety of American schools and colleges. In the first place there are the public schools and colleges supported by the state; then there are the endowed institutions. Of the endowed institutions, the first are the denominational, which were Protestant institutions in this country. Let me say here that a denominational school should command our respect. It enables parents to have their children brought up and instructed in that mode of teaching which they cherish. President Eliot then referred to the semi-denominational and the undenominational, or poly-denominational institutions, of which Harvard was the nearest example of the latter class, declaring that this form of institution is a precious one in American society.

He spoke strongly in favor of private schools, and declared that the privilege of parents to direct the education of their children is a most sacred one, and one of the most precious of human rights. Continuing, he said that the great variety of educational institutions in this country is of advantage, because of the wholesome competition which invariably arises among the institutions. Endowed and private institutions are freer and more flexible than the public schools. To make a change in a public school system requires the consent of a great many persons. The institutions that are leading the way at this moment in educational reform do not, as a general rule, belong to the public schools. The American public school is undergoing a new sort of trial. It has been forced, in my opinion, into an unnatural and untenable position. It has been forced into the position of secularization. It has been made to appear as a school from which religion is excluded. The Roman Catholic Church desires that moral and religious education go together. I do not believe that religion can be relegated to Sunday. And you cannot separate religion from history, science, philosophy. It is everywhere in human thought and speech. Let us apply to the American schools the same policy which the American State applies to the American Church—perfect freedom in all things and the enjoyment of many privileges, including exemption from taxation. Let the American public schools do likewise, and the great source of discord will be dried up in the American people. —*Boston Pilot, January*, 1892.

PROTESTANT TESTIMONY.

We find in the *Catholic Universe*, of Cleveland, of February, 1892, what follows:

Treating of the school question a short time ago, Rev. W. H. Platt, a Protestant minister of San Francisco, had the following to say:

"Secular schools may aim only at the Church of Rome but

THE GUN SHOOTS BACKWARD

and hits only the Church of the Protestant. Let the question come up fairly and squarely. Every citizen should be earnestly in favor of any system of education that includes religion, and as decidedly opposed to all that excludes it. Who is for pagan civilization over Christian civilization? The Puritans who settled the eastern part of this country were neither 'Jews, Turks, nor infidels,' but Calvanistic Christians. The cavaliers who settled Virginia and the South were of the English Church. The Roman Catholics were in Maryland.

It was Christian enterprise, Christian intelligence, Christian courage, and Christian money and blood which

FOUNDED THIS REPUBLIC,

and Christians claim a chief interest here. If we are in danger, it is from our own religious indifference, not from the growth of Romanism."

* * * * * * *

First—Secular schools in the interest of Protestantism is a fatal blunder. Protestantism no less than Romanism, needs for its influence and permanence the religious training of the young. Children are not born religious or moral, but are to be brought up " in the nurture and admonition of the Lord." Religion was a daily instruction with the Jews in their best condition. They were diligent to teach the commandments of God to their children, to talk of them as they sat in their houses and when they walked by the way, when they lay down, and when they rose up, and to write them on the posts of their houses, and on their gates.

It is not sufficient that the State educate during the six days of the week and the Church only one day. The Christian religion is a religion not only for Sunday, but for every day. Can the Church permit her children to live in the atmosphere of the world all the days of the week, have their associations with children of unbelievers, pursue their studies in schools where no positive religious influence confronts them, and expect all will be made right by an hour of religious instruction on Sunday?

* * * * * * *

Second—If secular schools were intended to destroy Roman Catholicity, they are signal failures. Protestants have honestly deluded themselves with the idea that secular schools, giving universal education and enlightenment (in which, in order not to offend any religious creed, even if they please none, religion should be excluded) would destroy the Roman Church. But do they do this?

WAS THERE EVER A GREATER MISTAKE?

They are unnecessary to keep Protestants out of the Roman Church, and they certainly do not convert the Roman Catholics into the Protestant Church. On the contrary, as they educate the young in no religion, but out of all churches, they destroy the Protestant Church, not the Roman. That church makes the most of its circumstances, but never abdicates its mission.

* * * * * * *

It is alleged that the three contestants for the control of our civilization are Romanism, Protestantism and Secularism. As to Protestantism, it is only a question of time when our present system of public schools will render it a dead factor.

* * * * * * *

Third—If secular schools are designed to break down all religion, they are a crime against civilization. It is not venturing too much to say that society will see, in the end, that while these schools were not so intended, they will have the effect, and are even now used by the enemies of religion to undermine faith and establish general scepticism. Protestantism has already felt their chilling influences. The Jews favor them because they let Christianity, which they hate tremendously, alone; the infidel favors them because they insiduously break down all religion, from whose discipline he resolves to escape; the Protestant favors them because, he thinks, they destroy the power of the Roman Church, and secular enlightenment is better than Roman ignorance. But this Protestant mistake is a fatal one. The sword is not even two-edged. It has but one edge, and it is drawn across the heart of Protestantism. Rome has nothing to do with these schools, but carries on her own institutions all the same as if secular schools did not exist. The whole bearing of this mistake is on Protestantism, and yet Protestants seem unable and unwilling to see it.

On the first of February, 1892, the Methodist ministers of Rochester and neighborhood discussed the question of denominational schools. Apparently, their praise was in favor of denominational education for the favored classes in academies, seminaries and colleges. When John Wesley left the university and city churches he went among the miners, and wherever the poor were to be found, to bring them all the religion he had himself.

www.ingramcontent.com/pod-product-compliance
Lightning Source LLC
Chambersburg PA
CBHW030243170426
43202CB00009B/603